The Riddle of the Sphinx

FRONTISPIECE. An antique cameo from Florence. A caduceus of Hermes with one serpent between twin serpents supporting an egg of rebirth. Above is a crescent moon between two sun-symbols. The cabalistic values of the letters in the field are as follows: Y = 700, P = 8, I = 10, A = 1. 700 (Y) + 8 (P) = 708 which is 2 × 354 (days). A lunar year is 354 days. 10 (I) + 1 (A) = 11 which is the number of days discrepancy between a lunar and solar year. 354 + 11 = 365 (days). The icon illustrates the calendric function of Hermes. From C. G. Jung, *Symbols of Transformation*, 1956, Bollingen Series XX, Princeton University Press, Princeton, N.J.

The Riddle
Of the Sphinx

CALENDRIC SYMBOLISM
IN MYTH AND ICON

CHARLES F. HERBERGER, PH.D.

Efstathiadis Group S.A.
Agiou Athanasiou Street.
GR - 145 65 Anixi, Attikis

ISBN 960 226 383

© Efstathiadis Group S.A. 1994

Printed and bound in Greece by Efstathiadis Group S.A.

To Melvina

"The collective memory stores
under the form of 'ornament'
or 'decorative' element, archaic
symbols of purely metaphysical
essence. The great part of
popular ornamentation is of
metaphysical origin."

—*Mircea Eliade*

Contents

List of Illustrations

Note of Acknowledgment

Every effort has been made by the author and publishers to locate the source of each illustration reproduced and to give due credit, but in a number of instances this has not been possible. The publishers and the author wish to express their appreciation for the use of all of the illustrative material. Grateful acknowledgment is made to the following publishers and others for the reproduction of illustrations or for permission to quote:

Cambridge University Press for passages, figures and plates as follows: from Arthur Bernard Cook, *Zeus, A Study in Ancient Religion*, 1964, *Vol. I* pp. 343-344 and pp. 412-413, *figures:* 332, 340, 341, 342, 343, 243, 562, 565, 323, 76, 330, 331, 329, 356, 355 and *plates* IV, VI, XXIV. *Vol. II figures:* 892, 658, 659, 915, 916, 589, 291 and 287. Hirmer Fotoarchiv, Munich: from Ludwig Drees, *Olympia,* 1968, *plates* 3a and 3b and 44. The Clarendon Press, Oxford: from V.E.G. Kenna, *Cretan Seals,* 1960, illustrations from p. 20, p. 36, p. 55, p. 56, p. 68, p. 69. The Meriden Gravure Co., Meriden, Conn: from Helen Wace, *Mycenae Guide,* Fifth Edition, 1969, illustrations from p. 14 and p. 21. Biblo and Tannen, Inc., New York: from Martin P. Nilsson, *The Minoan-Mycenaean Religion,* 1971, *figure* 196. The University of Chicago Press: from Emily Vermeule, *Greece in the Bronze Age,* 1967, *plate* XXVI. Cambridge University Press: from L.J.D. Richardson, "The Labyrinth", *Proceedings of the Cambridge Colloquium on Mycenaean Studies,* 1966, *figures* 1 and 6. Princeton University Press: from C.G. Jung, *Symbols of Transformation,* 1956, *figure* 43. Gregg International, an imprint of Avebury Publishing Company Limited, England:

from Marc Cameron and Sinclair Hood, *Sir Arthur Evans' Knossos Fresco Atlas,* 1967, *plate* IX, Second Version. Editions "Cahiers d'Art," Paris: from Christian Zervos, *L'Art en Grece,* 1946, *plate* 142. Editions "Tel", Paris: from *Encyclopedie photographique,* No. 16, 1937, *figure* C, p. 165. Philosophical Library, New York: from Charles F. Herberger, *The Thread of Ariadne,* 1972, *plate* IV and *figures* 2, 8, 18, 23, 24, 27. *Figures* 41 and 42 of this work are from photographs of unknown source.

Introduction

The contemporary fascination with the subject of mythology is a significant sign of our times—a veritable symptom of the *Zeitgeist*. This fascination is the resultant of two converging vectors in the modern cultural situation. On the one hand, a multitude of specialized scientific and scholarly studies, starting from widely separated points of origin have unexpectedly arrived at a common center in mythology. On the other hand, the spiritual wasteland of today's industrial society has awakened a deeply intuited need in man to rediscover his soul as a vital reality. This need has found expression in the arts, and especially in literature, in an assimilation of primitive motifs and mythical themes in the most experimental and representative contemporary works.

Let us look briefly at the scholarly branch of conversion. If one were asked to select from the vast number of scientific and scholarly works which have appeared since the mid-nineteenth century, those few which have exerted a maximum influence upon modern culture and society in the arena of ideas, certain obvious contenders would come to mind. Darwin's *Origin of the Species* would certainly be one, and Marx's *Das Kapital* would quite as certainly be another. A third of comparable stature, although not a single book, would be the collected works of Sigmund Freud. And I venture to suggest that a fourth contender in this very select league would be Sir James George Frazer's *The Golden Bough*.

An interesting parallel obtains here in that Darwin's work sets forth a theory of organic evolution, Marx's work a theory of socioeconomic evolution, Freud's a theory of psychic evolution, and Frazer's a theory of religio-mythic evolution. I cite Frazer in this company, not to imply that his work is the most important or conclusive in the field of mythology, but rather to suggest that as an influential book it invites comparison with the others and places the study of mythology among the leading intellectual concerns of our time.

Of course Frazer's work is but one thread in a web of significant studies leading to a center in myth. This is not the place to review the many contributions of these specialized studies. What is pertinent is to point out that they come from such various quarters. We have the immense contributions of modern archaeology—particularly prehistoric archaeology—as a storehouse of icons providing clues to the unrecorded mythology of various early cultures. Linguistic research has cracked the code of numerous ancient scripts such as Egyptian hieroglyphics, cuneiform, Hittite, and Greek Linear B, revealing a wealth of previously hidden recorded mythology. Cultural anthroplogy and comparative religion have shown us the links between ritual and myth in ancient cultures and existing primitive societies. Philosophy has contributed by analytic studies of the nature of symbolic forms and their genesis and, hence, thrown light on the symbology of myths. Art historians have traced the iconography of visual motifs to mythic origins. Recently even astronomy has come into the field by demonstrating that prehistoric monuments such as Stonehenge and others were used for accurate astronomical observations connected with seasonal rituals and, therefore, indirectly with myth. In literary criticism a stimulating and enlightening new approach to the interpretation of symbols, genres, structural forms, and plots has emerged of late by the discovery that literature had its origin in myth and that mythic patterns are discernible in great works of literature down to our day, even in many where a mythic theme was not the deliberate conscious choice of their creators. Finally, depth psychology has found in myth an expression of the dynamics of the unconscious brought to the light of consciousness symbolically, either in the personalistic sense as with Freud or in the collective and archetypal sense as with Jung and Neumann.

Now let us return to the other line of convergence—the creative innovators in the arts. The appeal and influence of non-naturalistic—and hence, symbolic—primitive art and sculpture to such artists as Gauguin and Picasso and many others is well known. Of course the plastic aesthetic freedom of African or Melanesian masks, idols, ritual paraphernalia, and the like exerts a charm in its own right. But we ought not to overlook the fact that most of this primitive art served a ritual purpose for its makers and reflected their mythic sense of the world of the spirit.

Since music is the most abstract of the arts, the tendency in this medium is not as obviously apparent. Yet it can be seen in such works as Stravinsky's *The Rite of Spring,* a composition inspired by primitive ritual, and in Milhaud's *Eumenides* with its overtones of Greek myth. The experimental pantonal music of Schönberg reflects the tendency in a different way. I can not say whether Schönberg was in any way influenced by the music of primitives, but at least the deliberate abandonment of the traditional single tone organization is an attempt to sweep away the layers of historical convention to get at something primordial beneath.

In modern literature the tendency toward the mythic is striking for the frequency with which it appears, the international distribution of examples, and the stature of the writers who have taken this direction. T. S. Eliot's *The Wasteland,* which derived its mythic nucleus from Jesse L. Weston's *From Ritual to Romance,* became a point of new departure for a whole generation of poets. In his own way, James Joyce pursued the same course with increasing intensity from the myth of Daidalos in the *Portrait* to a structural adaptation of the *Odyssey* in *Ulysses* and finally to an archetypal mythic dream in *Finnegan's Wake.*

William Butler Yeats drew from Irish mythology and folk tales and from a personal "vision" of a mythic character. His countryman, Bernard Shaw, in his typically cerebral fashion, deliberately set out to write a series of plays to replace the Pentateuch of the Bible. In France, Albert Camus found in the myth of Sisyphus a paradigm of the dilemma of modern man, while in Germany Thomas Mann turned to the Bible for his *Joseph* series, and Herman Hesse found in the life of Buddha the essence of his theme for *Siddhartha*. In Greece, Nikos Kazantzakis boldly picked up the thread of Homer's *Odyssey* as the starting point for an epic poem in which Odysseus becomes a mythic, yet distinctly modern hero. Saul Bellow's protagonist in *Henderson The Rain King* is a despairing American suburbanite who is regenerated by participation in a primitive ritual of a remote African tribe. And John Updike in *The Centaur* brings the Greek gods to life in a small Pennsylvania town. It would not be difficult to cite further examples, but this should suffice to call attention to the thrust toward myth in modern literature.

My contention, then, is that myth is everywhere being rediscovered, both as a clue to the psychology of primitive man—and, hence, to the quintessence of what is fundamentally "human" in all of us—and as a path to the vital regeneration of the spirit. My aim in this book is to add a modest contribution to that collective effort from yet another quarter of the horizon.

It is not generally recognized what a central role calendric symbolism played in the formation of classical mythology and its cultural offshoots. This is understandable for a number of reasons. Much of the symbolism inherent in classical mythology had its origin in the context of the pre-Olympian religion of the various peoples who inhabited Greece and the Aegean basin in the Bronze Age. Despite local differences, this religion was invariably oriented around a sacred calendar which regulated the ritual festivals of the seasonal and astronomical year. And since ritual determined the secret meaning—known only to initiates—of the verbalizations known later as mythology, the myths which arose naturally contained a great many symbols and motifs of calendric significance. This sacred calendar—the greater mysteries of which were known only to a select priesthood—was almost totally lost or submerged in the series of Dorian invasions that brought an end to the high civilization of Mycenaean Crete and Greece around the end of the second millennium B.C. Hence, the calendar and its hidden symbolism was lost to all but a few, who appear to have secretly retained a knowledge of some of its elements, to judge from the traces of it in the mystery cults and in the cyclical arrangements of the Olympic and other festival games at the dawn of the classical era.

When classical mythographers came to record in writing their inherited web of myths, the symbols and stories had been largely reinterpreted and in many cases modified or overlaid with new elements to adapt them to the Olympian religion which we know as classical mythology. Nevertheless, a great many calendric symbols—including significant calendric numbers—survived in Olympian mythology as written by men who were totally ignorant of their calendric connections. In addition, the conservative craftsmen who decorated pottery or engraved seal stones and so forth with mythic motifs frequently maintained as traditional, certain elements of calendric symbolism the significance of which they were not aware of.

For these reasons it is not surprising that modern scholars, ignorant of the existence of a Bronze Age calendar, to say nothing of its secret symbolism, and approaching classical mythology almost exclusively through written myths when interpreting visual icons, remained so long unaware of the calendric symbols underlying the surface.

There is, indeed, one notable exception to this generalization. Robert Graves in *The White Goddess* and *The Greek Myths* infers the existence of a Bronze Age solar-lunar ritual calendar in Greece and provides abundant evidence of calendric ritual symbolism to be found in both myths and icons. However, Graves lacked a concrete example of such a calendar in either graphic or written form and therefore could only conjecture its probable structure, numerical relations, astronomical basis, and symbolic associations.

Graves inferred that the Minoan Cretans must have had "a calendar based upon patient astronomic observation."[1] He was looking in the right direction. In *The Thread of Ariadne: The Labyrinth of the Calendar of Minos* (1972) I presented the evidence which led me to the conclusion that the well-known Toreador Fresco (c. 1500 B.C.) from the Palace of Minos at Knossos in Crete is, in fact, an accurate solar-lunar calendar in graphic symbolic form. My interpretation of this calendar shows that it functioned as a center around which the entire fabric of Minoan ritual and myth revolved.

My focus in that book was confined to a Cretan context, but as my research proceeded I became increasingly aware of corresponding calendric symbolism in myths and icons from beyond the confines of Crete and in duration of time, leading down to the classical period and in some cases even beyond. I was eventually compelled to the conclusion that the Mycenaean Greeks of the mainland and other ancient peoples of the Mediterranean area shared ritual calendars which, if not identical with the Knossos calendar, certainly had much in common with it. From this material supplemented by further research, the present book evolved.

My aim is to demonstrate the surprising prevalence of calendric symbolism in myths and icons where this significance has previously gone undetected and where the Knossos calendar provides the necessary clues. The intention is simply to provide selected representative examples of this symbolism so that when parallels are encountered elsewhere, they may be detected for what they are. In addition it will be shown how the ritual calendar became a nucleus around which a set of related archetypes constellated and composed an orderly and organically related whole.

This set of archetypes was inductively arrived at by observation of the evidence of their repeated association with the calendar, rather than on the basis of any arbitrary or theoretical assumption about the nature of archetypes. If they bear any relationship to the archetypes of mythology as delineated by Jung and Neumann, as in some instances they do, this is fortuitous rather than intentional. That archetypes do exist in mythology I find to be a fact. But their nature and genesis still appears to me to be a matter of tentative theory. I have therefore preferred not to make a priori assumptions about them but rather to let them speak for themselves.

My structural plan for this book is dictated by the archetypes of the calendar and their sequential arrangement. My method is to compare parallel examples of the archetypes chosen from both mythic and iconographic sources whenever this has been possible. In such comparisons it frequently happens that the myths help to explain the icons, while the icons in turn illuminate the myths. Indeed, where calendric symbolism is concerned, it is usually the icons which are the more revealing. An iconographic tradition does not require literacy or writing for its preservation. Images, motifs, designs, and symbols of primordial age may be retained as conventions by generation after generation of craftsmen long after their original significance has been forgotten. The surviving literary tradition of classical Greece goes back no further than Homer and Hesiod (c. 800 B.C.), while the iconographic tradition, preserved in the durable medium of the potter, the sculptor, the seal engraver, and the painter goes back to the Bronze Age. It is with a fresco painted by some unknown artist of the Bronze Age in the Palace of Minos at Knossos that this book must begin.

The Riddle of the Sphinx

CHAPTER I

The Knossos Calendar

In *Ecclesiastes* we find these memorable words:

> To every thing there is a season, and a time to every purpose under the heaven: A time to be born, and a time to die; a time to plant, and a time to pluck up that which is planted; a time to kill, and a time to heal; a time to break down, and a time to build up; a time to weep, and a time to laugh; a time to mourn, and a time to dance; a time to cast away stones, and a time to gather stones together; a time to embrace, and a time to refrain from embracing; a time to get, and a time to lose; a time to keep, and a time to cast away; a time to rend, and a time to sew; a time to keep silence, and a time to speak; a time to love, and a time to hate; a time of war, and a time of peace.[1]

I begin this book with these words because they express the mythopoeic sense of time which is my central theme—a riddle proposed by the Sphinx which we shall endeavor to solve. Our modern sense of time—shaped as it is by our scientific vision of the world—is radically different. We think of time as a mathematical abstraction, as a dimension of the universe, as a relative of another abstraction called "space." For us time is secular. We say, "Time is money." And utilitarian. "Time is of the essence." And linear. "Progress." Unless, of course, we are in a poetic mood.

1

As this book will show, man's earliest sense of time was conceived in a poetic mood. For him time was a metaphor. That is to say he conceived the reality of time through images and symbols which were at once concrete and palpable yet universal in their implications. Hence, metaphors. Even numbers were for him metaphors. They were like the five fingers of the hand or the five phases of the moon, but never simply "5," a mathematical abstraction. For him time was not secular and utilitarian, but sacred and numinous—a divine mystery. And above all it was never linear, progressive—going somewhere in a hurry. No, it was circular, rhythmic, always returning upon itself and never in a hurry. "A time to be born, and a time to die; a time to plant, and a time to pluck up that which is planted."

Within the frame of this vision of time, man's earliest calendars evolved. They were ritual calendars that marked the ever recurring rhythm of life and death—for the crops and herds, for man, and for the cosmic gods. And rhythm, of course, leads to counting, even if one is counting in a circle. The mathematical aspect of the calendar was made possible by the act of counting, but counting, and hence, mathematics remained within a mythopoeic frame of reference.

The earliest evidence that science has as yet discovered of man's ability to count is very early, indeed. This evidence appears first in the Upper Paleolithic period (c. 30,000 B.C.). Alexander Marshack, after microscopically examining bones engraved by men of the Old Stone Age, has concluded that the sequential marks on these bones are notations for counting. And if Marshack's theory is sound, Stone Age man was counting the five phases of the moon, complete lunations, and seasonal spans in days.[2] It is not difficult to see how a lunar calendar could eventually evolve from such beginnings.

The next step would naturally be to count the circle of the sun, that is the number of days in a solar year. How early this was accomplished we do not know with certainty. A Danish scholar, Tons Brunés, has set forth a theory that a Megalithic stone ring at Erdsvagg in Norway was used to locate the position of the setting sun at the solstices and the equinoxes of the solar year.[3] Such a ring could be used as a

2

primitive calendar permitting the days of the year, the half year, and the quarter year to be counted. Brunés does not attempt to date this Megalithic ring.

There are, of course, many such Megalithic rings in the British Isles. Professor Alexander Thom has made an extensive study of many of these rings using modern surveying instruments. He concludes that a number of them were used for astronomical calendar calculations. The most frequent alignments he discovered were for sunset at the solstices and for Martinmas and Candlemas. Martinmas falls at the midpoint between fall equinox and the winter solstice, and Candlemas falls at the midpoint between the winter solstice and the spring equinox. Alignments for both the equinoxes also appear in some rings. The solar alignments are the most frequent, but he has also found some lunar alignments, primarily for full moon nearest the solstices.

Dating these Megalithic rings with accuracy is problematic. Carbon 14 dating of some of them indicates a range from 3200–2000 B.C. for solar alignments. For the lunar alignments, moon astronomy indicates a range from 1930–1750 B.C. Thom believes that the days between these stations of the year were counted and that consequently an accurate calendar was achieved, possibly as early as the third millennium B.C.[4]

Of course, the most famous of all these stone rings is Stonehenge. Recently an astronomer, Gerald S. Hawkins, has made an extensive study of the alignments at Stonehenge using computer methods. The great number of accurate alignments—solar, lunar, and stellar—which he verified by mathematical means and astronomical observations leave no room for doubt that Stonehenge was used as an astronomical observatory and also as a computer of eclipses. Stonehenge was built and added to in stages covering a period from c. 1900–1600 B.C. according to Hawkins's dating.[5]

Obviously such an observatory as Stonehenge could provide the necessary knowledge upon which an accurate calendar could be based, and in a sense the monument was itself a calendar. And I believe we may safely infer by analogy with other ancient calendars elsewhere that it was certainly a ritual calendar and religious ceremonies would have taken place there.

In fact, there is a passage derived from the work of the Greek historian, Hecataeus (sixth century B.C.), which alludes to a round temple on the island opposite Gaul, where the inhabitants, the Hyperboreans, worshiped Apollo or in other words, the sun. Hecataeus says that the Hyperboreans, "the people beyond the North Wind," were ruled by priests, performed ritual dances, and honored Apollo's nineteen-year cycle, i.e. the Metonic cycle which reconciles solar and lunar time every nineteen years.[6] Hecataeus makes it clear that he is speaking of a very ancient tradition; therefore, if the reference is actually to Stonehenge, as it appears to be, it could be the pre-Celtic Stonehenge of the Bronze Age.

We may be reasonably sure that the people of Stonehenge had a ritual calendar as early as the second millennium B.C., but we can only conjecture its structure and relation to ritual. But by virtue of records preserved in cuneiform, we know at least the basic structure of the Sumerian calendar and the later Babylonian calendar derived from it. Both were ritual calendars regulating the sacred year. The Sumerian system came into being some time during the third millennium B.C.

The Sumerians and the Babylonians appear to have been the first people who attempted to reconcile solar and lunar time. This problem arises because if one begins to reckon from a New Year festival, falling, let us say, on a day when the winter solstice coincides with new moon, twelve average lunations, or a lunar year, will amount to 354 days, while the solar year ending with the winter solstice amounts to approximately 365 days. Therefore, there is an 11-day discrepancy between the lunar and the solar year. This discrepancy increases to 22 days in two years and 33 days in three years.

Now it is evident that one can reconcile the solar and lunar New Year approximately by intercalating a thirteenth month of 30 days at the end of three years. But this reconciliation is only approximate—not only because a 3-day discrepancy remains and will increase in time, but also because the solar year is actually closer to 365.25 days. Neither the

4

Sumerians nor the Babylonians succeeded in solving this problem in a systematic mathematical way. What they did was simply to observe the heavens and when the astronomers were sure that a thirteenth 30-day month needed to be intercalated, they informed the king and the king authorized an extra month by royal decree. The records show that these intercalations were not made at any regularly recurring intervals, but irregularly and empirically as the situation seemed to demand.[7]

The Egyptian system, which is also of great antiquity, disregarded actual lunations and divided the lunar year into twelve official "months" (moons) of 30 days each for a total of 360 days. The five remaining days of the 365-day solar year were not considered a part of the official year. They constituted a five-day New Year festival honoring the five divinities—Osiris, Horus, Set, Isis, and Nephthys.[8] This meant that their official "months" showed no integration with observable lunations any more than our months of the modern calendar do. Furthermore, since their total solar year was 365 days and failed to intercalate a day every four years (leap year) to keep the season in phase with the solstice, their fixed calendar festivals gradually moved further and further away from their appropriate places in the seasonal year.

However, after a cycle of 1,460 years, which they called a Sothic Year, the accumulated fragments of this discrepancy amounted to a whole year which they then intercalated in the annals. This was celebrated by a special festival and it appears to have been the origin of the myth of the Phoenix, the mysterious bird which rises reborn from its own ashes from a nest in a palm tree every thousand years.[9] In other words, a Sothic Year died and was reborn.

It is apparent, then, that none of these early calendar systems succeeded in establishing a regularized and consistent method of intercalation to reconcile solar and lunar years. Unless, of course, the people of Stonehenge had done so on the basis of the nineteen-year solar-lunar cycle, but this remains unknown.

There is, however, another way of reconciling solar and lunar years. It is an astronomical fact that if one begins

5

counting from the coincidence of a new moon on the winter solstice, exactly eight years will elapse before a new moon will again appear on the winter solstice. This eight-year cycle occurs because ninety-nine average lunations closely approximate eight solar years. Now if we assume that there are twelve months in a lunar year, in eight years we would have a total of ninety-six months. But, in fact, ninety-nine average lunations will have occurred. Hence, if we should intercalate a thirteenth thirty-day month at the end of each of three regular intervals within the eight year cycle, we would have ninety-six plus three months or ninety-nine months. This would give us a regularized perpetual system for reconciling solar and lunar years, except that we ought also to account for leap year by intercalating a single day every four years.

Now a system of this kind was used by the Greeks of the classical period for regulating pan-Hellenic religious festivals such as the Olympic and Pythian Games. On the other hand, for secular matters the independent city-states had calendars which differed widely in the naming of months and the position of the official New Year. If we depend strictly upon written records, it appears as if this eight-year solar-lunar system sprang into being suddenly and without any prior development about the eighth century B.C.

Martin P. Nilsson in his book, *Primitive Time-Reckoning* (1920), found this sudden appearance of a fully developed solar-lunar calendar with a regular system of intercalation unaccountable, since no such system could be found that early in Egypt or Babylonia or elsewhere. He writes,

> When history begins, the Greek time-reckoning as we know it appears: it is a lunisolar year with named lunar months, in which the intercalation is cyclically regulated, so that in a period of eight years (*Oktaeteris*) a month is three times intercalated, viz. in the 3rd, 5th, and 8th years. This appearance of an ordered form of year and a cyclical intercalation is completely unprepared for.

And he concludes,

In my opinion the Greek calendar cannot be explained from premises originating in the country itself, and therefore cannot have arisen of itself in Greece.[10]

If such a calendar did not arise in Greece, where did it come from? Nilsson could offer no satisfactory answer to this question. Robert Graves, who was aware that some such system must have existed in Mycenaean times, judging from traces of it in the symbolism of Greek mythology, thought that it must have come from the high civilization of Minoan Crete. He infers that the Minoans must have had "a calendar based on patient astronomic observation."[11] However, when Graves wrote this sometime prior to 1955, no direct evidence of the existence of a calendar in Minoan or Mycenaean times had as yet been discovered.

Then in 1955 Michael Ventris and John Chadwick published their first edition of *Documents in Mycenaean Greek* which summarized the findings derived from the deciphering of the Linear B tablets from Knossos and Pylos. The tablets which recorded religious offerings to the deities, and *only these tablets* by the way, revealed the names of months both at Knossos and at Pylos. Six and possibly seven month names were identified on the Knossos tablets and two or possibly three month names appeared on the Pylos tablets. Here, for the first time, appeared written evidence that a Bronze Age calendar existed at both Knossos and Pylos and that it was not merely a utilitarian system but a ritual calendar. Ventris and Chadwick write:

> Both Furumark and Meriggi have recognized from the month-names which introduce each tablet that the series forms part of a ritual calendar, specifying or recording offerings sent to a limited number of places, priests and divinities.[12]

Furthermore, one of the Knossos month names strikingly corresponds with a month name in the Arcadian calendar of classical times.[13] It appears, then, that the Pelasgians of Arcadia had a calendar which had something in common with the Knossos calendar. This points to a solution of the problem raised by Nilsson as suggested by Graves, that the solar-lunar calendar of classical Olympia was derived from the Minoan calendar of Knossos. It appears to be an inheritance from the high Bronze Age passed on to the classical Greeks by the Pelasgian inhabitants of the central Peloponnese, the Arcadians.

There was, indeed, a solar-lunar ritual calendar in use at Knossos in the Bronze Age. In *The Thread of Ariadne: The Labyrinth of the Calendar of Minos,* I have presented the evidence leading to the conclusion that the so-called Toreador Fresco from the Palace of Minos at Knossos contains in its border a solar-lunar calendar graphically represented by symbols and numerical elements. This fresco dates from c. 1500 B.C., and my interpretation of its border symbolism reveals a solar-lunar system based on the eight-year cycle with three regularly intercalated months. As I have shown, it was a ritual calendar which provides the clue to the significance of a great many icons, motifs, and myths which make up the fabric of Minoan religion. The pre-Dorian Mycenaean Greeks inherited more than a mere abstract calendric system. The calendar and its religious context were one and indivisible. That this is so I shall demonstrate in the ensuing chapters. But first it will be necessary to explain the structural elements of the Knossos calendar in detail.

Since I have presented the evidence and reasoning which led to the deciphering of the Knossos calendar in *The Thread of Ariadne,* there is no need to repeat it here. The following discussion of the calendar is therefore merely an abstract, explaining how it is to be read. An explanation of the religious context in which it is embedded will also have to await a further chapter.

A diagram showing how the calendar may be read is provided in Figure 1 (p. 10). There it will be seen that the eight-year cycle begins on winter solstice and new moon on the outermost vertical left-hand track at a point five day-marks up from the base. Day-marks are counted on the tracks in accord with the direction of the arrows and the numbering of the tracks for years one through four. Four years is the length of a half-cycle, which then is repeated on the calendar to bring solar and lunar years together again at winter solstice and new moon at the end of a full cycle of eight years. The diagram also indicates seasonal periods and ritual festivals. The vertical tracks, which begin and end each year, represent the winter season with the winter solstice at its mid-point. The top horizontal tracks indicate the length of the spring season and the bottom horizontal tracks represent the summer season. There are four festival periods in each year, which are indicated on alternate tracks in alternate years. This arrangement was apparently necessary to keep seasonal lengths constant. A three-day spring festival, a three-day fall festival, and a five-day winter festival, immediately preceding winter solstice, are indicated. A table of seasonal and festival dates is provided in Figure 2 (p. 12).

Months were counted alternately as thirty and twenty-nine days in length and intercalations of a thirteenth thirty-day month were made at the ends of years three, six, and eight. And a single day was intercalated in track three every four years for leap year. As previously shown, this system brings the solar and lunar New Year together after ninety-nine lunations or eight solar years.

Plate 1 (p. 13) illustrates how moon phases and the days of the solar year were coordinated. Each lunation was divided into five phases, numbered on the diagram from 1 to 5. Phase 1 is new moon, phase 2, waxing moon, phase 3, full moon, phase 4, waning moon, and phase 5, dark of the moon. Only sixty of the sixty-two phases graphically represented on the calendar were counted in any single lunar year. The remaining two phases represent an overlap which indicates the directional reading of the sequences. The stationary moon phases on the calendar did not indicate the actually observable phase of the moon, because actual lunations vary in length while the calendar symbols are static. But collectively they did correspond mathematically with synoptic lunations (average months) and by their spacing in relation to the solar tracks, they indicated when a thirteenth month should be intercalated.

Plate II (between pp. 14 and 15) is a restoration of the extant fragments of the entire fresco, including the bull-vaulting scene within the borders, as restored under the direction of Sir Arthur Evans, who discovered it in his excava-

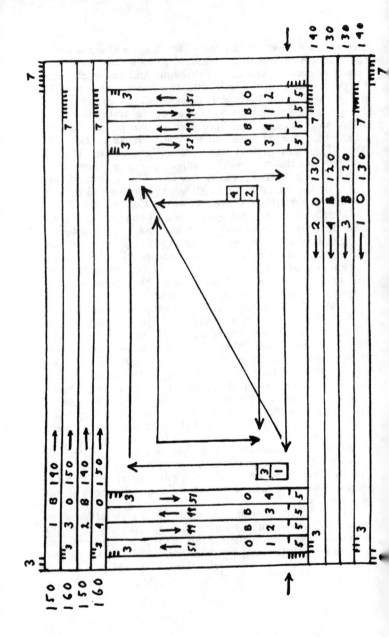

FIGURE 1. Schematic diagram of calendar. Key: Years 1 and 3 begin at the arrow at left and years 2 and 4 at the arrow at right. Year tracks are marked 1,2,3, and 4 and their color is indicated as B (blue) or O (orange). Total days counted in any track indicated within the track. Total number of marks on horizontal tracks indicated outside the appropriate tracks. Number of days in festivals and where they fall indicated by graduated marks on appropriate tracks. Arrows within frame indicate pattern of calendar sequence in four-year cycle.

FIGURE 2. Table of seasons and festivals.

Years 1 and 2

Dates	Season Length	Dates	Festival Length
21 Dec.–2 Feb.	43 days–Winter	3Feb.–5 Feb.	3 days–Spring Festival
6 Feb.–25 Jun.	140 days–Spring	26 Jun.–2 Jul.	7 days–Summer Festival
3 Jul.–30 Oct.	120 days–Summer	31 Oct.–2 Nov.	3 days–Fall Festival
3 Nov.–15 Dec.	44 days–Fall	16 Dec.–20 Dec.	5 days–Winter Festival

Years 3 and 4

Dates	Season Length	Dates	Festival Length
21 Dec.–3 Feb.	44 days–Winter	4 Feb.–6 Feb.	3 days–Spring Festival
7 Feb.–26 Jun.	140 days–Spring	27 Jun.–3 Jul.	7 days–Summer Festival
4 Jul.–31 Oct.	120 days–Summer	1 Nov.–3 Nov.	3 days–Fall Festival
4 Nov.–15 Dec.	43 days–Fall	16 Dec.–20 Dec.	5 days–Winter Festival
	44 days–Fall		
	(yr. 3–leap yr.)		

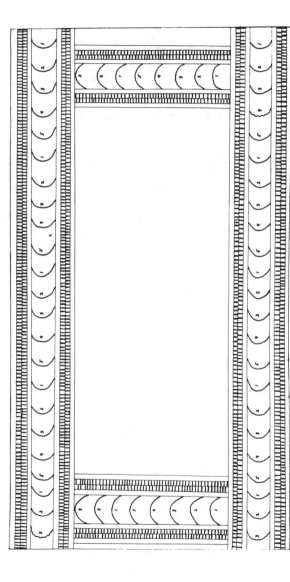

PLATE I.

tions at Knossos. This restoration in conjunction with the restoration of the extant fragments themselves in the Heraklion Museum provided the basis for the diagrammatic version illustrated by Plate I. The count of day-marks in each track, where fragments do not provide them, was estimated mathematically on the basis of average marks per inch in the particular track in question.

This much should suffice to explain the structural elements of the Knossos calendar and how it is read. But these bare bones are merely the skeleton of a calendar which in the mythopoeic vision of its makers was inseparable from a whole body of vital mythic associations. That living body of myth and image will be discussed in the next chapter.

PLATE II.

CHAPTER II

Calendar Archetypes

Man has in common with his animal brothers a physical evolution, but he is distinguished as man by having in addition a cultural evolution. Culture is strictly a human product, and man, its maker, is a creative animal. Culture began when man extended his given capacities by artificial means, or perhaps we should say artful means—the creative act. He extended the reach of his arms and legs by means of tools and weapons. In doing so, he projected himself beyond himself into the surrounding environment. Equally crucial to the birth of man as man was his extension of his spiritual capacities beyond what nature gave him by the creative act of symbol-making. Just as he gained command over his physical environment by the extension we call a tool, he gained command of his spiritual environment by the extension we call a symbol.

The symbol enabled man to project his unique human vision and values on the surrounding external world and thereby to make of it a realm where his spirit could feel at home. By making tools man secured his physical survival, and by making symbols he humanized his world and ensured his spiritual survival.

Man is man because he is a tool maker and a symbol maker, and I suspect that the two capacities came into being in concert. The tool itself was a creative idea and could not have been conceived without a prior mental perception of an

15

analogy. And thinking in terms of analogy is a principle of symbolism. The evidence of mythology supports this conclusion. In mythology the invention of tools is always attributed to a god or a culture hero. And what is significant is that the invention is often explained by a sudden inspiration based upon a perceived analogy. For instance, the Cretan culture hero, Talos, is said to have invented the saw by analogy with the backbone of a fish. And the God, Hermes, is said to have invented certain letters of the alphabet by analogy with the sticklike figures of a flock of cranes flying high overhead. The former is an instance of the invention of a tool and the latter of the invention of a symbol, but both depend upon the principle of analogy.

The mythopoeic world which we are about to explore is a world of symbols. And the surprising fact is that it is a very orderly world. But the kind of order it represents is different from the order of analytic logic. It is the order of mythopoeic synthesis. To perceive this order, one must understand the principles upon which it is based.

A clear understanding of the principles of synthesis can be achieved by contrasting them with the principles of analysis. Despite the complexity of which analytic thought is capable, it rests entirely upon three basic principles: the principle of identity (A is A), of contradiction (A is not B), and of the excluded middle (A is not both A and non-A).

This kind of thinking depends fundamentally upon a process of abstraction. When one says A is A, one is abstracting some entity from its context in reality and assigning it a fixed meaning, which thereafter may not be changed. In saying A is not B, one has taken a further step. If A has been abstracted from its context and assigned a meaning, any further thing abstracted from that context must be assigned a different meaning. Finally, when one says A is not both A and non-A, one is excluding the possibility of A meaning both what it was assigned when abstracted and in addition having a different meaning. In short, a double meaning for A is excluded.

Just as analytic thought is based on only three principles, so also is synthetic thought. But the principles are radically different. While analytic thought depends entirely upon abstracting entities from context, synthetic thought is concerned with the relations that things may have to each other within a given context.

The first principle of synthetic thought is analogy. Two or more images in a painting, let us say, are analogous because they share a similar shape, color, or position in the total composition. As images they remain concrete and separate, but they may be equated with each other because they share a common form. The meaning, therefore, of such an image in the painting is not single and fixed, but multiple and relative.

The second principle is the principle of polar opposition. The colors in our painting, let us say, are some of them light and others dark—or highlights and shadows perhaps. But the value or "meaning" of the light colors depends on their opposition to the dark colors, for, in a sense, darkness is the absence of light and light is the absence of darkness. The light areas in the painting do not "contradict" the dark areas. It is rather that each defines the other by being its polar opposite.

The third principle of synthesis is what might be called the principle of the included middle. To return to our painting, each element of the composition, be it image, color, texture, or whatever, is related to every other element in an organic synthesis, assuming, of course, that the painting is a proper work of art. Therefore we cannot remove any element or replace it with something else without affecting destructively the unity and harmony of the whole. Nor would any element in the painting have any significance by itself alone. In other words, the part is to the whole as the whole is to the part.

The important points to notice are that analysis deals with abstractions in isolation. Synthesis deals with concretions in context. In analysis meanings are single and unchanging. In synthesis they are multiple and relative, and therefore may change depending upon the particular set of relations in focus in a single act of perception. In analysis wholes are divisible and the whole can mean nothing more than the sum of its parts. In synthesis the whole is more than the sum of its parts, and the part may stand for the whole or the whole for the part. For instance, in poetry the figure of speech known as synecdoche is an image in which the part stands for the whole. We say, "Have you wheels?" meaning an automobile. Or the figure called metonymy in which the whole stands for the part. We say, "The White House declares," meaning the President declares.

The archetypes of the Knossos calendar make up a synthetic fabric where these principles apply. Therefore they can not be properly understood in isolation from each other. The context in which they came into being was Minoan religion and ritual and religions of parallel structure elsewhere in the Bronze Age.

This religion was dominated by a great goddess, who, despite her many names, can be identified as essentially one deity, being a complex of all that is feminine or the feminine principle itself. She was seen as the mother of all creation, and, hence, her nature is all-embracing, even to the point of containing all opposites. Since in mythopoeic thinking, the part may stand for the whole, she is the *omphalos,* the navel of the universe, whose mound-like shape is the world's womb, and whose spiral umbilical means not only the turn toward death, but the counter-turn toward rebirth. She represents the constant principle in the flux of being, which is ever changing, yet ever the same, a circle of eternal return.

Since she contains all opposites, she needs no male god as mate, much less as lord and master. Parthenogenetically, she gives birth to a semidivine child, her son, who, upon reaching maturity, becomes her spouse as a sacred king. The sacred king rules, but he rules in her name in a matrilinear society where inheritance is through the mother's line. The sacred king is associated with the seed and with male fertility. Whereas the goddess represents the constant principle in being, he manifests temporal change. If life is to be nourished, the seed and the fruit, the grain and the grape, must be cut or plucked, ground or crushed, and its flesh and its blood consumed. Hence, the sacred king must die. But after the harvest, the seed is buried in the ploughed fields and comes to life once more in the spring. The sacred king must die, but he is always reborn.

18

In the earliest times, the annual death and rebirth of the sacred king was probably celebrated in rituals at festivals falling in the autumn and the spring. We have seen that long before the Bronze Age, the cyclical nature of the moon was observed, the approximate number of days of a complete lunation was known, the phases of the moon were counted in days, and eventually the number of lunations in a seasonal year was discovered. From this knowledge a lunar year calendar evolved, and the rituals celebrating a sacred king's death and rebirth could be regulated accordingly. The moon, whose periodicity corresponds with the normal feminine menstrual cycle, was naturally associated with the great goddess. The calendar was, therefore, regarded as sacred from the beginning and its regulation of ritual and the reign of a sacred king placed it in the very center of the mythopoeic vision of life.

When the solstices came to be recognized, a true solar year was discovered and counted in days. Since the sun waxes in strength from the winter solstice to the summer solstice and then, in turn, wanes, the dying king, who is annually reborn, was easily associated with the sun and became a sun-king, spouse of the moon-goddess. The next step, as we have seen, was to develop a solar-lunar calendar to reconcile solar and lunar time. We know now that this had been achieved in Minoan Crete at least as early as c. 1500 B.C. if not earlier.

My study of the Minoan calendar and the icons and myths related to it in the Bronze Age, and in detectable traces long thereafter, reveals that the calendar constituted a nucleus around which a number of constantly recurring archetypes orbited. I use the term "archetype" to denote visual images or mythic patterns which may vary in specific manifestations but which embody analogous form and significance. These archetypes called attention to themselves by the frequency of their appearance in a calendric context and by their apparent interrelations. For my purposes, it is not necessary to accept or reject any particular theory of the genesis of archetypes in general, whether metaphysical, psychological, or whatever. The fact is simply that a number of archetypes are most apparent in association with the

19

Knossos calendar and we may now examine them in the context of Minoan religion and ritual. They are: (1) the twin kings, (2) the transcendent third, (3) calendar totem beasts, (4) the attendants upon the king, (5) circles of eternal return, (6) the labyrinth, and (7) calendric numbers.

The archetype of the twin kings derives from early ritual practice when the tribal fertility king was slain seasonally, either actually or mimetically, to ensure the welfare and fertility of the tribe, of their crops, and of their pastoral herds. He is a twin because his death is seasonal, for like the yearly harvested grain, the ripe seed of which was replanted, he dies only to be reborn as his twin, the succeeding seasonal king. And his death is necessary because by analogy with nature's rhythm, there can be no new crop without the reaping of the ripe ears and the burial of the vital seed in the earth.

The sacrifice was performed not in a superstitious effort to propitiate an angry and arbitrary divinity, in the later Greek and Roman manner, but in the realistic wisdom that *ex nihilo nihil fit*—out of nothing, nothing comes. If you do not sow, you cannot reap.

As we have seen, at a more advanced stage of astronomical knowledge, the king became associated with the yearly cycle of the sun and its twin polar stations at winter solstice and summer solstice. The sun's cycle, of course, brings about the seasonal change and, hence, the seasonal twins became solar twins, the king of the waxing sun, from winter solstice to summer solstice, and the king of the waning sun, from summer solstice to winter solstice. Each died and was reborn as his twin brother at the appropriate solstice.

As solar kings the twins were united in a sacred marriage with the great goddess as moon-goddess. With the development of the eight-year solar-lunar calendar, tribal kings could extend their reigns to four years, a half-cycle, or to eight years, a great year, and undergo a ritual death and rebirth ceremony twice yearly at the solstices. At such times, it appears that the king's totem beast, in Minoan Crete usually a bull, could be sacrificed as a surrogate in his place.

It also appears, from evidence which I have presented in *The Thread of Ariadne,* that the Minoan king at the period when the Knossos calendar was used, met his ritual death not at winter solstice at the end of the eight-year cycle, but at full moon of the seventh lunation following at a special fourteen-day festival in mid-summer.

In a subsequent stage in the development of some ancient calendars, a nineteen-year solar-lunar cycle was discovered, which permits an even closer reconciliation of solar and lunar years. This cycle was also an eclipse cycle. By adopting this as a great year, a sacred king's reign could be further prolonged.

The twin king archetype is well illustrated by an Early Minoan Age engraved seal from Milatos. (AM. 1938.764) The seal is a three-sided prism bead with related designs on its three faces. (Figure 3) One side shows the twin kings, who can be recognized as such by the fact that they are precisely the same in size and pose except that each is inverted in relation to the other, while each extends a hand to the other in greeting. This symbolically suggests their kinship as well as their opposition as twin aspects of the year. A second side repeats the archetype in a variant form as two identical fish. We shall later see that two fish, or more frequently two serpents, represent the twin kings specifically at the winter solstice. The two human twins on the same seal, therefore, probably represent their summer solstice meeting. The third face shows a totem beast, a Cretan wild goat, which is probably a theriomorphic emblem of them both as goat-kings. In the Early Minoan Age, the Cretan wild goat appears more frequently than the bull in association with the sacred king. As we shall see, this archetype has many further implications, but this brief discussion will serve to identify it.

The archetype of the transcendent third arises out of the twin king archetype. Since each king dies to be reborn as his twin, there is a necessary third stage of kingship in the life beyond death, which provides the link between the twins. This third transcends death to be reborn.

A good example of the transcendent third may be seen in the ritual depicted in the center of the Knossos fresco calendar. (Plate II) There we see a charging bull, the totem beast of the sun-king of the waxing year.[1] Before the bull is a female toreador between his horns, grasping them in a manner to gain leverage to make a vaulting leap between the horns and over the bull's back. In the center, above the

21

 FIGURE 3. Early Minoan seal from Milatos. Two tunny-fish, twin king motif, and Cretan wild goat. (19-38.764) *Ashmolean Museum.*

bull's back, is a male figure rendered in red, the conventional color for all males in Minoan art. He has already passed between the horns of the bull in a leaping somersault, his back arched and arms and legs extended so that his lithe body almost describes a circle. Behind the bull, a second female toreador stands with outstretched arms ready to catch the vaulter, who will, when he alights on his feet, be in a position with hands outstretched for balance, which duplicates her stance.

This ritual, which took place at the summer solstice festival, was a mimesis of death, of life after death, and of rebirth. The red male figure, representing the sun-king, goes between the bull's horns, the "gates of horn," known in later Greek mythology as an entrance to the abode of the dead. He goes to a death union with the goddess, a kind of sacred marriage, but in the life beyond death. His circular position represents this stage. It is circular because his death will eventually be followed by his rebirth. When he completes this circle, he will be received by the female toreador behind the bull, who represents the goddess and his rebirth through her. The female toreador between the horns of the bull indicates that he also went to his death in honor of the goddess. The bull, of course, is the theriomorphic form of his twin, and probably was sacrificed as a surrogate for the king of the waxing year who must die at summer solstice. The sun-king in the arched or circular position represents the transcendent third. As we shall see, there are other images which can also represent the archetype of the transcendent third, but this should suffice to clarify its significance.

A third archetype consists of calendar totem beasts. Under primitive tribal conditions, a clan or tribe and its chief identify themselves with some element or creature of the world of nature—an animal, fish, plant, tree, insect, or even a particular mineral. This totem creature or beast is mythopoeically experienced as the ancestor of the chief and the tribe. They share the *mana,* or life-potency, of the totem beast and it is taboo to eat of its flesh, except on certain festivals when it is ritually slain or sacrificed and then partaken of as a communion, parallel to the Christian Eucharist. In partaking of the flesh or blood of the totem beast, they share its *mana* and are revitalized.

These ritual associations appear in the Bronze Age in a somewhat modified form. In the period of the Knossos calendar, the bull represents the sun-king in the spring season, the season of the waxing sun. As many Cretan seals show, another beast, the lion, pursues the bull, usually in a circular motif, and kills his prey. An example may be seen in Figure 4. (AE. 1230) As I have shown elsewhere, the lion was equated with the sun-king in the summer season and he kills the spring-bull at the midsummer festival.[2] A third calendar beast is the serpent, which, however, usually appears in icons as two serpents. In the Knossos calendar, serpent season begins with the fall festival and ends with the spring festival. It is the winter season of the sun, split at its mid-point by the winter solstice and a five-day festival. The solar-serpent dies and is reborn at the winter solstice which halves this season, and appropriately we have two serpents or twins to mythically suggest this duality. And, of course, the fact that snakes shed their skins and emerge as if reborn, as well as the fact that their flexibility permits them to take their tails in their mouths, and thereby suggest eternal return, were associations not overlooked by the mythopoeic mind.

One additional calendar beast, the Eagle-Griffin, appears in this Minoan group. (Figure 5) The Minoan Griffin usually has an eagle's head and wings, a lion's body and paws, and a serpent's tail. She is feminine, like the Sphinx, her counterpart, and represents the moon-goddess in her death aspect, for it is at the five-day festival, corresponding to the five phases of the moon, that she takes the life of one serpent, and at winter solstice, following the festival, bestows life on his twin. These five days, which at the end of every great year coincide with the dark of the moon, are hers alone. The official solar year was made up of the remaining 360 days just as it was in the Egyptian calendar previously discussed.

FIGURE 4. Cretan seal from a tholos tomb at Hagia Pelagia. Bull-lion circle motif. (AE. 1230.) *Ashmolean Museum*.

FIGURE 5. Griffin motif.

. The Griffin is tripartite because, as a representative of the great goddess, she rules all three seasons. She is sometimes represented as slaying a bull or with a bull's skull between her lion's paws, and therefore we may infer that she rules bull season, as well as lion season and serpent season.

There are, of course, variations on these beasts as we have already seen. In the Early Minoan period, two fish, like the astrological sign of Pisces, appear to antedate the two serpents, and a Cretan wild goat appears in icons where later we more frequently find a bull. Archaeological evidence indicates that the Minoan people were of mixed stock and that they did not arrive in Crete in a single migration. Furthermore, until the Late Bronze Age, it appears that most Minoan cities were politically autonomous. Therefore, we should expect to find different totem beasts representing the sacred king in differing ancestral groups. And, of course, even a single city could undergo changes of clan totem. For instance, the myth of the coming of the Goddess Europa from Phoenicia to Crete on the back of a bull may reflect some such change. Be that as it may, it is the archetypal pattern of calendar totem beasts with which we are at present concerned, rather than the variations.

A fourth archetype takes the form of a group of attendants upon the sacred king or kings. The origin of this archetype can be traced to tribal initiation ceremonies. In a tribal social organization, all the critical steps in human life that call for adjustment to change are induced collectively by *rites de passage* which make these experiences meaningful by relating the individual to the collective experience of the tribe as a whole and to the greater whole of nature itself, which also suffers periodic but meaningful change. Thus birth, puberty, procreation, old age, and death are each shown to have their proper time, and their own special dignity, and are sanctioned by poetic archetypes which are beyond time itself in the primordial world of myth. In Minoan Crete, such rituals were held periodically on the calender festivals of the year, synchronized in significance with seasonal change, and celebrated publicly by the sacred priest-king, by a priestess representing the great goddess, and by a band of attendants upon the king, who essentially represented the tribe as a whole—much as the chorus in Greek drama represented the people of the state in relation to their king.

Although there are no written accounts of Minoan date to verify with precision the nature of these rituals and their timing, it is sufficiently clear from the evidence of art, architecture, and the Minoan calendar that they were observed, and they left their traces in myth, in literature, and the religious festivals of the Greeks and other peoples of later times. The band of attendants upon the sacred king can be recognized in the Curetes, whom Rhea provided as attendants upon the infant Zeus in the Dictaean Cave.

According to the Greek myth, Cronus, father of Zeus, promptly swallowed his children as soon as they were born. To save Zeus from this fate, Rhea gave Cronus a stone wrapped in swaddling clothes to swallow, and secluded the infant Zeus in the Dictaean Cave in Crete where she provided him with the Curetes as attendants, young armed men who danced about the child shouting and clashing their spears on their shields to drown out his wailing lest Cronus hear it and find him.[3]

The myth is a later variation upon the tribal ritual origin of such a band of youths, but it is enlightening in certain details. No doubt Cronus swallowed his children lest they succeed him as king by matrilinear succession. The Curetes beating their shields are performing a ritual dance in celebration of the rites of birth, the birth of a semidivine king. For the early Cretan, Zeus-Zagreus was not the immortal Olympian of later times, but a dying fertility god incarnate as a sacred king.

We are seeking the archetype which is only partially reflected in this myth. There are many other parallels to the Curetes such as the Titans, the Dactyls, the Corybantes, the Telchines, the Cabeiri, the satyrs and maenads, and others. What emerges as common to them all is that they are celebrants of initiation rituals or *rites de passage,* are attendants upon a god or sacred king, and are representatives of a collective initiation in which the whole tribe or its appropriate age and sex groups participate. Such initiation rituals have usually three stages: a mimesis of death, a trial or test, and a symbolic rebirth. This archetypal pattern is psychologically appropriate because it induces acceptance of necessary

27

change in the conditions of temporal life. For instance, young men and women who have attained marriageable age must "die" as children, be introduced to the mysteries of sexual maturity, and be "reborn" as responsible adults.

Such rituals were collectively performed by mimetic dances in the Theatral Area at Knossos and in the great central court of the Palace of Minos, as extant frescoes and seal engravings show. And it is evident that both men and women participated in them. The trial or test aspect of initiation is plainly discernible in the athletic contests and games, which Minoan art shows were held at certain ritual festivals of the year. There is clear evidence of boxing and wrestling matches and of expert tumbling being performed. But the most sensational of these events, which were at once athletic games and ritual ceremonies, was the bull-vaulting pictured in the Knossos calendar as previously discussed. This much should suffice to clarify the archetype of the attendants on the king.

The archetype of eternal return is of high frequency in Minoan iconography as, indeed, it is in many early cultures. Although it may be representated by a variety of images and in relationship to other archetypes, what is essential is that it suggests the cyclical nature of time and change and the timeless in the temporal. We have already encountered it in the circular position of the bull-vaulter, where it is in the context of the archetype of the transcendent third. It is also naturally associated with the great goddess because she is the constant principle in nature, complete in herself and all encompassing—the eternal One.

One such image is the spiral. Beginning with the Early Minoan Age, the spiral is constantly to be found on seal stones, sealings, and pottery. It occurs in a multiplicity of variations and combinations—basic coils, running spirals, S-spirals, C-spirals, triple and quadriple combinations, and in naturalistic forms such as octopus tentacles, and conch and murex shells.[4]

In addition to the spiral, other examples of the archetype of eternal return in Minoan art are the swastika, the triskelion, the circle, the meander, and the five-pointed star or endless pentad. The latter is rendered as a star with an interwoven outline, so that it may be followed with the eye in an endless sequence (Figure 6). It is interesting to note that it became in classical times the badge of the secret order of the Pythagoreans. It was for them a symbol of the timeless in the temporal, of the five elements, the five senses, and of health and wholeness.[5] Still another example of the archetype which is frequent in Minoan art is the double-bladed sickle motif (Figure 7). All of the above variations on the archetype appear frequently in a context of other calendric symbols, which is not surprising since it is essentially an emblem of the cyclical nature of time.

FIGURE 6. Drawing of motif of a clay sealing from Phaistos (c. 2000–1700 B.C.) In classical times, this pentagram was adopted as the badge of the Pythagoreans. HM. Gallery III, Case 40, No. 781. *Heraklion Museum.*

FIGURE 7. Early Minoan Age prism bead from North Crete. Double bladed sickle motif. (AM. 1910.244.) *Ashmolean Museum.*

Another frequent version of this archetype is what I call, for lack of an established term, the bull-lion circle motif. It features a lion, or sometimes a lion-man, in pursuit of a bull-man or Minotaur in a circular or torsional design. An example may be seen in Figure 8. (AM. 1938.1069) The seal shows us the fabled Minotaur, who is both sacred king and solar-bull. He is pursued, and will be slain at the summer solstice by his twin, the man-lion, the calendar beast of the summer season combined with a human form—and both spin together in a circle of eternal return. Thus, the archetypes of the twins, the calendar beasts, and of eternal return appear in concert.

FIGURE 8. Late Minoan engraved gem from Crete. A man-lion pursuing a man-bull. Bull-lion circle motif. (AM. 1938.1069.) *Ashmolean Museum*.

We have seen that the circular position of the bull-vaulter in the Knossos calendar connoted death and rebirth of eternal return. It is surprising to see how early this motif appears in Minoan art and the context in which it appears. An Early Minoan seal from Hagios Onuphrios (HM. 12) displays this motif. Like most seals of this early period, it renders figures in a simplified linear fashion, but if we examine it closely, we can interpret the pictorial content (Figure 9). The seal has a circular hole in the center indicating that it was probably strung on a cord and worn suspended from the neck. It features a man with his back arched in a somersault position and disposed about the central circular hole. There are also other images in the field. In the upper left corner is a crescent moon, no doubt representing the moon-goddess. Since the human figure appears to hold the circular hole in his hand, it probably represents the sun; therefore, he would, accordingly, represent the sun-king.

FIGURE 9. Early Minoan amulet from Hagios Onuphrios. Sun-king in arched position of a bull vaulter. (HM. 12.) *Heraklion Museum.*

The remaining objects in the field are so schematically rendered as to be problematical. However, I take the object below the crescent moon to be horns of consecration, a well-known Minoan altar symbol, and the V-shaped symbol below it is possibly the feminine pubic triangle, a reference to the sacred king's marriage with the goddess. The long curved object at the bottom of the field is probably a fertility bough, a usual attribute of the sacred king. The object to the right of it is shaped very much like an almond. The almond is to this day a crop tree in Crete and seal stones of this shape were common in Minoan times. The almond, being a seed, is a male fertility symbol. The most significant feature of the seal, however, is the sacred king arched backward in a simulation of the circle of eternal return.

Let us now look at an example from the Late Minoan

31

Age when improved glyptic technique makes figures easily identifiable. A skillfully engraved seal of Late Minoan II date (AM. 1938.1071) shows a Minotaur with back arched and his human legs dangling, so that they nearly touch his bull's head (Figure 10). Under his arched back is a figure-of-eight shield, a well-known symbol of the Minoan sacred king. Between his head and heels is an impaled triangle, here unmistakably a symbol of the union of the king with the goddess. The Minotaur is plainly enough the solar bull-king who dies yearly and is yearly reborn in a circle of eternal return.

FIGURE 10. Late Minoan gem from Psychro Cave. (AM. 19-38.1071.) Man-bull in circle of eternal return with figure-of-eight shield and impaled triangle. *Ashmolean Museum.*

Another example from the same period, Late Minoan II, is enlightening because it features a calendar beast in the same position. (AM. 1938.1058) As Figure 11 shows, the beast is the lion of the summer season. He is also arched backward, as if performing a somersault. Lion season in the Minoan calendar begins at the midsummer festival, and this is the festival in which the bull-vaulting ritual occurred. The bull-vaulter in the Knossos calendar is, therefore, by mythopoeic analogy, a ritual representative of the lion-king of the summer season, who will kill the bull-king of the spring season at this summer solstice festival.

The sixth archetype is the labyrinth, an archetype so

FIGURE 11. Cretan seal of Late Minoan II Period. Lion in arched position of bull vaulter. Circle of eternal return motif. (AM. 1938. 1058.) *Ashmolean Museum.*

rich in multiple significance that it is difficult to decide from which angle to approach it first. But its calendric significance may be most appropriately considered last since it is an archetype around which all of the other archetypes are constellated.

Although the Cretan Labyrinth is the most famous, there are other labyrinths mentioned by various ancient authorities. In the first century B.C., Strabo visited the Egyptian Labyrinth near Lake Moeris by the Nile. He describes it as an elaborate maze incorporating the tomb of the Egyptian King Imandes. He was told that it contained a chamber for each of the provinces of the Egyptian kingdom at the time of the reign of Imandes and that the priests and priestesses of the various provinces assembled there for religious rites.[6] Imandes has been identified as Amenemhat III of the twelfth dynasty and therefore the tomb dates c. 1849–1801 B.C.[7]

Strabo also mentions Cyclopean labyrinths (i.e. of Mycenaean date) near Nauplia in Argos and describes them as "caverns."[8] According to Pliny, there were also labyrinths on Samos and Lemnos and the early Etruscan king, Lars Porsena, had one built as his royal tomb.[9] Most of these labyrinths appear to have been royal tombs incorporating mazes of some kind and frequently also underground or concealed chambers. In one sense, then, the labyrinth was emblematic of the chthonic underworld and the house of the dead. This significance is also borne out by Vergil, who in

33

describing <u>Aenaeas'</u> descent to the underworld by way of the cave at Cumae, tells us that the entrance gates were carved in relief by Daidalos with an image of the Cretan Labyrinth.[10]

As I have shown in *The Thread of Ariadne*, the labyrinth image in Minoan art is a quadrangle inscribed with crossed diagonals, which evolved from the image of a double axe placed between bull's horns or their equivalent, the "horns of consecration," which appear on Minoan shrines and altars. Figure 12 illustrates by a comparison of seal designs how the labyrinth motif of a quadrangle with crossed diagonals is derived from the *labrys*, or double axe between the horns of the sacred bull. This also explains the name "labyrinth" which was so called because it takes its shape from the *labrys*.

The double axe, in turn, was the sumbol of the Minoan great goddess, who was mistress of the Labyrinth or Potnia Dipu$_2$ ritojo, "the Lady of the Labyrinth," as a Linear B tablet from Knossos calls her.[11] The *labrys* was a sacrificial axe with two crescent-shaped blades, emblematic of the last phase and the first phase of the moon-goddess. And since the waning crescent, after the dark phase of the moon, gives birth to the new moon crescent, one significance of the double-bladed axe is that the solar kings who die by it will be reborn. The two blades, which cut both ways, will slay the solar-bull and the solar-lion in turn, but each are yearly reborn in a circle of eternal return. Therefore the labyrinth is not only a symbol of death, and life after death, but of the rebirth or reincarnation of sacred kings. And this is probably why the royal tombs mentioned above were called labyrinths.

Another essential feature of the labyrinth archetype is its complexity as a maze. In Minoan art this aspect is implied in many ways, but most frequently by spirals, zigzags, serpentine patterns, meander patterns, and checkerboard patterns. Homer, describing the shield of Achilles in the *Iliad,* says that it pictured youths and maidens engaged in a complicated spiraling dance on a "dancing-floor like that which Daidalos once fashioned in spacious Knossos for Ariadne of the lovely hair."[12] This complex dance, which was probably performed in a ritual celebration of a festival in the

34

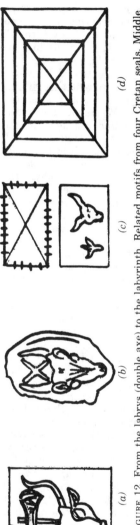

FIGURE 12. From the labrys (double axe) to the labyrinth. Related motifs from four Cretan seals. Middle Minoan III—Late Minoan Age. From Knossos and vicinity. (a) (HM.337) (b) (HM.152) (c) HM. Gallery II, Case 28, No. 1786. (d) HM. Gallery V, Case 65, No. 2180. *Heraklion Museum.*

Theatral Area at Knossos, appears to have been a choreographic mimesis of the courting of the moon-goddess by the sun-king in the maze of the labyrinth. This conclusion is supported by Lucian who, in listing traditional Cretan dances, mentions a dance known as the Labyrinth.[13] A similar maze-like dance is mentioned by Vergil in the *Aeneid,* who says that Aenaeas brought this ritual dance to Italy as a heritage from Troy.[14] Furthermore, in many places in Europe as far apart as Wales and northeastern Russia, maze patterns have been found marked out on pavements and used by country folk for a traditional labyrinthine dance known in some places as the "Troy Dance."[15]

But what is the significance of the maze aspect of the labyrinth? We have seen that the labyrinth is emblematic of the chthonic underworld of the dead, in one sense, but that it also implies rebirth. The great goddess is an earth-goddess and the dead are laid to rest in the earth. But it is also from the womb of the earth-goddess that sacred kings are reborn. Is the maze of the labyrinth, then, an emblem of the womb?

There is a remarkable Etruscan labyrinth pictured on an *oinochoe* which unmistakably supports this equation (Figure 13). It pictures two horsemen engaged in what is apparently an equestrian version of the "Troy Dance." They emerge from a crudely circular maze which in its shape is even biologically like the womb. The womb-like labyrinth is plainly marked in Etruscan letters "Truia" or "Troy." But the truly convincing sign that this labyrinth is equated with the womb is the figure of a little partially developed fetus, crouched as if yet unborn, which is placed above one of the horsemen. Clearly this associates the horseman with one who has not yet emerged from the labyrinth of the womb.

He carries a shield bearing the emblem of a partridge. Myth tells us that Talos, whose mother's name was Perdix, meaning "partridge," was thrown from the Acropolis by his uncle, Daidalos, who was reputed the designer of the Cretan Labyrinth. But Athena saved the soul of Talos by turning it into a partridge in mid-air. In *The Thread of Ariadne,* I have identified Talos as one of the twin kings of the year at Knossos. His association with a partridge stems from a ritual mazelike dance in imitation of the hobbling courting dance

36

of the cock-partridge.[16] If we fit together these clues, it becomes apparent that the horseman identified with the partridge and the fetus is a sacred king who has been ritually slain by his twin at a seasonal festival and who has become a fetus once more, to be eventually reborn from the womb of the labyrinth. His soul, however, has been saved by the great goddess and transformed into a partridge.

FIGURE 13. Figures on an Etruscan *oinochoe* from Tragliatella. Seventh century B.C. Twin horsemen and a fetus emerging from a labyrinth labeled "Troy."

His twin, the horseman behind him, is armed with a spear, the sacrificial weapon, and his shield bears the emblem of a duck. The great goddess sometimes has as her bird of epiphany a swan, a goose, or a duck. Leda, for instance, who was courted by Zeus in the form of a swan, gave birth to the famous horsemen twins, the Dioscuri, who were a Greek version of this same archetype. This horseman, then, is obviously the tanist who slays his twin in a yearly festival and his shield bears the drake as spouse of the goddess as duck.

The other side of this wine jar adds to the story. It pictures the ceremonial procession preceding the sacrificial death of the sacred king. He is escorted in a sun-wise arc by a priestess and seven men, each armed with three spears and carrying shields with a boar device. Behind them follows the tanist with a single spear. He is led into the presence of a commanding figure, a chief-priestess of the moon-goddess, who holds out to him an apple, a passport, like the apples of the Hesperides, to immortality. As a counter gesture, he holds out to her an egg, which spells his rebirth after the ritual slaying.[17]

The seven men, each armed with three spears, and the tanist armed with a single spear pose a problem. We can expect the numbers here to have calendric significance because the scene represented is plainly the death of a sun-king at the hands of his twin at a calendar regulated ritual. The numbers are 7, 8, and 22. That is, there are 7 men and the tanist makes 8 and the total number of fatal spears is 22.

The ancient Etruscans had a solar-lunar calendar, for traces of it are evident in the later Republican Roman calendar, which had its roots in Etruscan tradition. But the working structure of the Etruscan calendar is, for the most part, unknown. The Etruscans, or at least some of them, appear to have come to Italy from somewhere in Anatolia, probably Lydia or Lycia, at some time in the eighth century B.C.[18] At any rate, their close connection with the culture of the Bronze Age Aegean is plain. Their calendar appears to me to have had some things in common with the Knossos calendar, but also to have differed in some respects. I shall set forth my views on this problem in my last chapter, but here I shall content myself with a few brief identifications.

The number twenty-two is a solar number, being the number of days in a solar division of the year into sixteen parts. The number seven is a lunar number which alternates with eight as a division of the days of the month, in such a way as to make lunar and solar divisions of the year coincide. This occurs because seven days plus eight days make fifteen days or half a month and thus, full moon. This is the Etruscan *Idus* later known as the Roman *Ides*, the fifteenth day of the month. Continuing the alternation by adding seven days, we get twenty-two days, which coincides with the solar division of the year into sixteen parts of twenty-two and twenty-three days alternately. Finally, by adding the next alternate, eight days, we get thirty days or a full month.

The important thing to note, however, is that while the labyrinth is in one sense a womb and in another sense a

38

ritual dance, both senses tie together in relation to the calendar. In *The Thread of Ariadne*, I presented the evidence which leads to the conclusion that the fabled Labyrinth of King Minos at Knossos was not the royal palace, but the fresco calendar itself and, hence, also the sanctuary where its secrets were guarded.

This equation may be plainly seen if we compare the labyrinth motif as illustrated in Figure 12 with the diagram of the fresco calendar in Figure 1. The motif of a rectangle with crossed diagonals, sometimes including graduated marks on the borders, is repeated in the calendar by the alternately spiral and serpentine pattern by which the calendar is read, and by the day tracks on the borders. The bull-vaulting ritual depicted in the fresco, as it has been shown, is mimetic of death, life after death, and rebirth, which is entirely consistent with the labyrinth as thus far interpreted, as well as with its calendric meaning.

The memory of the original significance of the labyrinth as a calendar lingered at Knossos well into the classical period. Coins of Knossos from c. 500 B.C. onward represent the labyrinth as a maze-like swastika. Two coins in particular show identical maze-like swastikas, one with an eight-rayed sun disk and the other with a crescent moon at the center of the maze (Figure 14). The placement of these two symbols in the center of a labyrinth points to a traditional association of the labyrinth with an eight-year solar-lunar calendar cycle in the city where both the labyrinth and the calendar originated.

We have discovered, then, that the labyrinth takes its name and shape from the *labrys*, or double axe, that it is both the underworld of the dead and the womb from which the dead are reborn, that it is evoked by a ritual dance performed in a maze-like pattern, and that all of these aspects combine in its significance as a ritual calendar.

It is also apparent that a whole constellation of other archetypes fall into orbit around this central symbol—the twin kings of the year, the transcendent third, the calendar beasts, the ritual attendants on the king, the circle of eternal return, and symbolic calendric numbers. Thus the labyrinth is an all-inclusive archetype, having both spatial and temporal significance. As tomb, womb, and underworld, it is spa-

FIGURE 14. Four coins from Knossos of the fifth century B.C. Above, the labyrinth as a swastika with symbols of the sun and the moon in the center. Below, the labyrinth as a maze. This maze, which takes eight turns to reach the center, is structurally the same as the maze on the Tragliatella *oinochoe*. Compare Figure 13.

tial, but as solar-lunar calendar, it represents the cyclical nature of time—the ritual dance of the sun and the moon, the alternations of the seasons, and the collective human experience of birth, maturity, mating, death, and rebirth. Finally, by uniting spatial and temporal modes in a higher synthesis, the labyrinth archetype suggests transcendence of space and time and becomes a mandala of wholeness.

The last complex of archetypal character to be discussed consists of symbolic calendric numbers. Inevitably we have already encountered calendric numbers in defining the other archetypes. But certain fundamentals of this complex remain to be discussed.

Both the Knossos calendar itself and a great deal of evidence from Minoan iconography at large show that odd

40

numbers were sacred to the great goddess and considered feminine, while even numbers were sacred to her consort and considered male. Although all odd numbers were essentially feminine, those most frequently encountered in a context that relates them to the goddess are three, five, seven, and eleven, and multiples thereof, and, of course, also one since the goddess ultimately unites all things in unity.

In the calendar, three is her number as the three seasons symbolized by the Tripartite Griffin and also by the three-day spring and autumn festivals. Five is her number as moon-goddess, reflected by the five phases of the moon and by the five-day festival at the winter solstice. Seven is the number of days in the summer solstice festival, and it is at full moon of the seventh lunation following the end of a great year, that the sacred king's reign came to an end. Seven is therefore a moon-number and, accordingly, signifies the goddess. Eleven and its multiples are her numbers because the lunar year ends eleven days before the solar year, and this makes necessary the periodic intercalation of a thirteenth month.

The even numbers most frequently associated with the sun, the twin solar kings, and the male principle in general are two, four, eight, and twelve, and multiples thereof. Two, of course, stands for the solar twins of the year. Four represents the number of years in a half-cycle of the calendar and its four day-tracks. Eight, of course, is the number of years in the full solar-lunar cycle. Twelve is a solar number and male, because there are normally twelve months in the year, except the years of intercalation, which have thirteen months, a feminine number, honoring the moon-goddess.

Also, as previously mentioned, the official year had only 360 days, the remaining 5 days of the winter festival being outside the sun's year and presided over by the goddess as Griffin. Now 360 is the product of the solar number 12 × 30, 30 being a moon-number, since it equals the number of days in a month. Furthermore, the 360-day year was neatly divided into twelfths (3/12, 4/12, 5/12) by the length in days of the three seasons of the sun. For all of these reasons, twelve is a solar-number and male.

There are other calendar numbers of significance but this discussion should be sufficient to clarify the archetypal complex, the others being deducible from the calendar itself. We are now acquainted with the Knossos calendar and the archetypes that cluster around it. Equipped as well with a synthetic vision of how the archetypes relate to each other mythopoeically, we may now venture to let the Sphinx ask us what riddles she will.

Chapter III

The Riddle of the Sphinx

When Oedipus arrived outside of Thebes, he encountered the Sphinx on Mount Phicium. The Sphinx was a monster with a woman's head, an eagle's wings, a lion's body, and a serpent's tail. She had been sent by the mother-goddess, Hera, to plague the Thebans in reprisal for an offense against fertility which Laius, the aging king of Thebes, had committed. He had, in fact, made Chrysippus, an attractive young boy, his catamite and abducted him. The Sphinx accosted any man on the road to Thebes and demanded the solution of a peculiar riddle which had been taught her by the Three Muses. Many a man had failed, and as a consequence had been torn apart on the spot and devoured by the Sphinx. In fact, Queen Jocasta's own nephew, Haemon, whose name means "bloody," failed the test and the Sphinx proved the name "bloody" appropriate, indeed.

When Oedipus arrived, fresh from the slaying of King Laius, she halted him and asked this question: "What being, with only one voice, has sometimes two feet, sometimes three, sometimes four, and is weakest when it has the most?"[1] The humanistic mythographers of the classical period tell us that Oedipus answered, "Man, because he crawls on all fours as an infant, stands firmly on his two feet in his youth, and leans upon a staff in his old age." A rather pedestrian answer to so mysterious a riddle! If Oedipus had really given so lame an answer as this, he would have been dispatched forthwith. But Oedipus was the son, or rather adopted son, of a sacred Mycenaean king of Corinth, Polybus, and consequently was initiated in the secret calendar mysteries which governed sacred kingship in the Bronze Age. And since we know that he succeeded in answering the riddle, his answer must have been, "Helios, the sun, for though the sun is one god and speaks with one voice, he runs an eight year course with his queen, the moon-goddess, and to keep in step with her for an eight year cycle, he is equivalent to ninety-nine moons, he must go on three feet twice and halt for her to catch up, on two feet once and halt for her, and on four feet twice and halt, and he is weakest on four because he is so little ahead of her then in their race that he need only wait a day, whereas at the other times he is thirty days ahead of her."

The key to the explanation lies in the eight-year solar-lunar calendar. The sun and the moon must begin and end their race in step—that is when new moon and the winter solstice coincide. But since a lunar year of twelve lunations is eleven days shorter than a solar year, it is necessary for the sun to take three steps and halt, as it were, at the end of the third and sixth years when an intercalation of a thirteenth month will bring solar and lunar years nearly in phase again. Hence, the sun goes sometimes on three feet. A third thirty-day intercalation is necessary after only two further solar years, that is at the end of the eighth year which ends the cycle. Hence, the sun sometimes goes on only two feet. But it is also necessary to intercalate a single day once every four years, or on leap years, and this occurs twice in eight years. Accordingly the sun sometimes goes on four feet, but is weakest then in the sense that he is only one day ahead of the moon.

Now the Sphinx was a calendar beast like the Minoan Griffin. She was composite because she represented the sacred union of the sun and the moon and the transformations which the sun went through in the seasons of the year. Others of her kind were the Chimera, a she-goat with a lion's head and serpent's tail, and the Phoenix, who arose from its own ashes every thousand years, a symbol of a thousand-year cycle.[2]

She has a woman's head because she represents the

great fertility goddess, the spouse of the sacred king. Her lion's body, eagle's wings, and serpent's tail are emblematic of the three seasons of the year. The agricultural year in Greece has only three seasons, spring, which in prehistoric Thebes was probably bull season, summer, which was probably lion season, and winter, which would have been serpent season. This would correspond with the season-beasts of the Minoan calendar. Like the Minoan Griffin, the Sphinx does not embody any physical part of a bull. Her eagle's wings represent the goddess as bird of prey, the destroyer or death-bringer, who takes the life of the old-year king at the five-day winter solstice festival. But in Crete the spring was certainly bull season and it is likely to have been so also in Thebes, because Cadmus founded Thebes where a moon-cow he had been following lay down and his sister, Europa, had been abducted by a solar bull. The Sphinx was sent by Hera, originally a moon and fertility goddess, to punish the impiety of Laius, who apparently had developed a taste for young boys. The three Muses, who provided her riddle, were the goddess again in triad.

It is not surprising that Oedipus should be asked a question by the Sphinx which tested his knowledge of the sacred calendar mysteries, which she, in the name of the goddess, represented and guarded. And it is appropriate that she took her station on a mountain, since mountain caves—such as the Idaean and Dictaean caves in Crete—were the shrines where she was most anciently wont to be worshiped. Unlike the princely Oedipus, who had slain the king who must die, the other aspirants to the throne of Thebes did not know the secret and were therefore sacrificed, dismembered, and eaten, as surrogates for the sacred king were ritually sacrificed and eaten in the most primitive stage of these cults. Kingship in the Bronze Age, as we have seen, depended upon matrilinear succession because the human queen was usually the high priestess of the mother-goddess and represented her dominance. Accordingly one could only become a king by virtue of marriage to the reigning queen or, in some cases, her youngest daughter. Furthermore, it was necessary for the young king to actually slay the older king whom he replaced.

Now Oedipus, although he knew not who it was, killed

Laius, the former king—and according to the myth, his own father. And since he passed the test imposed by the goddess, he was permitted to marry the queen, Jocasta, and by this union with his mother—again unknown to him—became the succeeding sacred king of Thebes. And so was his destiny, as prophesied by the oracle at Delphi, which in the Bronze Age was the very voice of the great goddess herself, fulfilled. Such is the calendric and ritual meaning of this very ancient myth—the later interpretations of Sophocles and Freud notwithstanding.[3]

We have examined the mythic tale of Oedipus and the Sphinx in the light of calendric symbolism with interesting results. Now let us look at a visual icon representing the same incident. In the Vatican Museum in Rome is a ceramic wine cup, a *kylix,* dated c. 480 B.C. which depicts Oedipus solving the riddle of the Sphinx (Figure 15). The Sphinx with her lion's body, eagle's wings, and serpentlike tail, perches on the capital of an ionic pillar. She has the head of an attractive young woman and a coronet crowns her hair in honor of the goddess she represents. The pillar is also symbolic of the goddess since we know that she was worshiped in pillar shrines in Minoan Crete, the stone pillar being a variation on her sacred tree of life. Oedipus, wearing a broad-brimmed hat and holding a knobbed staff, sits before her on a large mound-like stone. He wears the himation over his left shoulder, which was generally the token of royalty, and he sits in a pensive fashion with a hand under his chin and his left leg crossed over his right knee so that his left foot is off the ground.

Despite the casual appearance of his pose, beautifully caught by the ceramic painter, every detail in this image is symbolic. The broad-brimmed hat is of a kind frequently worn by Hermes in Greek art of this period (Figure 16). Oedipus is about to solve an obscure riddle and he wears the "thinking-hat" of Hermetic wisdom. His knobbed staff is a variation on the fertility bough, traditionally an attribute of sacred kings. The mound-like rock upon which he sits and ponders is an allusion to the *omphalos,* the sacred navel-rock at Delphi, which is the source of oracular wisdom, born of the earth-mother. But the most telling detail is that his left foot makes no contact with the ground.

FIGURE 15. A red-figured *kylix*. Oedipus solving the riddle of the Sphinx. *Vatican Museum*, Greek vase collection, Case K, No. 13 (16541).

Everyone knows that Oedipus' name means "swollen foot" or "club-foot." But it is less generally known that sacred kings of his type in myth and icon almost invariably have a vulnerable sacred heel—such as Achilles had—which in ritual practice must never be allowed to touch the earth. We shall see more of this motif later, but now it is only necessary to point out that it clearly identifies Oedipus as a sacred king and consort of the goddess.

So far it is apparent that the ceramic artist was in some way in touch with the ritual significance of his subject. But is there any hint of the calendric meaning of the riddle? Let us look closely at the remaining details of the design. Behind

FIGURE 16. Relief sculpture, (c. 450–440 B.C.) Hermes, wearing the *Petasos* and carrying the *Caduceus*, confronts Aphrodite, who expresses her love for him by holding forth a blossom and a figure of Eros.

the pillar upon which the Sphinx perches is what appears to be merely an ornamental design filling what would otherwise be an aesthetically disturbing empty area in the total composition. It does, indeed, serve this aesthetic purpose, but is that all? It consists of two opposed stylized three-petaled flowers and two opposed S-spirals, one of which is tipped with a brush remarkably resembling a lion's tail. In Minoan and Mycenaean art, the three-petaled lily is constantly associated with the great goddess and the spiral is as constantly associated with the death and rebirth of the sacred king. If we count the functional members of this design, we find that the number three appears twice—the two three-petaled lilies—the number two appears once—the two S-spirals—and the number one appears once—the lion's tail—but this occurs in a context of four, since the opposed flowers and spirals make a design of four elements.

It is obvious that the artist—or rather the Sphinx—is giving Oedipus a clue to the solution of the riddle, for the design is a paradigm of the calendric secret. The significant numbers are three—twice, two—once, and four associated with one. The formula is a lunar intercalation at the end of the third, sixth, and eighth years, and a single day intercalation at the end of every four years.

We have yet to examine the circular border design. It is comprised of running spirals separated at intervals by exactly eight crosses. This is hardly surprising since it is an eight-year solar-lunar cycle that provides the clue to the riddle. The spirals suggest the eternal return aspect of a cyclical calendar in which the sun dies yearly at winter solstice and is thereupon reborn. And it is worth noting in passing that the New Year was celebrated in Thebes in Boeotia at the winter solstice, as in Minoan Crete, even in classical times when most cities in Greece had adopted a different station of the year for New Year.[4]

We have in this ceramic work a consistent combination of meaningful calendric and ritual symbols which closely parallel our interpretation of the literary myth and support its validity. Was the ceramic painter aware of the original meaning of the riddle, or was he merely following an antique graphic convention in depicting Oedipus with the Sphinx while in ignorance of its implications? We cannot know with certainty. The latter alternative is more probable. I have found time and time again that visual icons can tell us more about the original ritual origin of myths than the literary versions. This is true because the myths in written form are relatively late, while the iconographic tradition frequently reaches back into the Bronze Age. Moreover, some written myths took their origin from a misinterpretation of icons.

Myth preserves another riddle of the Sphinx which is interesting in relation to the one asked Oedipus. The riddle is "Who are the two sisters who give birth to one another?" The classical mythographers believed that the answer was "Day and Night," because in Greek both words are feminine in gender, and day and night follow each other in sequence.[5] This philologizing answer was surely the invention of a literary mind of the classical period. The correct answer must have been "The new moon and the old moon crescents."

49

The moon was a goddess and her maiden phase as new moon crescent gradually increases until as pregnant full moon she gives birth to her sister, the waning crescent, who in turn once more gives birth to the new moon. This sequence of moon phases equated with young and old aspects of one goddess is an integral part of the Knossos fresco calendar. The Minoan moon-goddess's double axe with its two opposed crescent blades is another version of the same motif. Since the Sphinx was mistress of a solar-lunar calendar and since the answer to the riddle Oedipus solved was "the sun," the answer to this riddle is certainly "the moon."

A festival honoring the moon-goddess in Attica, which was still celebrated in classical times, parallels this interpretation of the riddle in significance. On the sixteenth day of the month of Mounichion, which was the last month of spring of the Attic calendar, cakes called *amphiphontes* were brought to the sanctuary of Artemis and to the shrine of "Hecate at the cross-roads." The original meaning of the ceremony, although still performed, appears to have been forgotten by classical times, to judge from the fact that classical writers could not agree on its significance.[6] Now *amphiphontes* means "shining on both sides" in Greek. The festival takes place on the sixteenth of the month, which means at the middle of a lunation, at least ideally, and therefore at full moon. The ceremony honors two goddesses, who even in classical times retained their original association with phases of the moon—the virgin, Artemis, as new moon crescent and the hag, Hecate, as the old moon crescent. When is the moon "shining on both sides?" Obviously at full moon when the festival takes place honoring the two moon-sisters, who represent the alternately visible sides of the moon, each of which gives birth to the other. And, of course, it is at this point, full moon, when Hecate as moon is "at the cross-roads" for the moon is about to stop waxing and begin waning. We may now return to the riddle of the Sphinx and give a more particularized answer. "Who are the two sisters who give birth to one another?" The answer is Artemis and Hecate.

One of the titles of Artemis was "the younger Hecate," and Hecate was sometimes described as tripartite in body and three-headed, her heads being that of a lion, dog, and mare.[7] Hecate was also mistress of the three-headed dog,

Cerberus, the guardian of the underworld.

Her three bodies, three heads, and her three-headed dog were variants on the tripartite Sphinx and represented a three-season year.[8] Her name itself appears to be derived from the Greek word for "one hundred," which in round numbers probably refers to the ninety-nine lunations of the eight-year solar-lunar calendar. Hence the Sphinx, in posing a riddle about Hecate, is really asking a question about her own mythic significance.

Hecate, as the last phase of the moon, was the great goddess in her death aspect and her abode was the underworld. This appears to be a pre-Hellenic tradition, for the Olympian mythologists made Hades and Persephone rulers of the underworld, although they retained Hecate and her dog, Cerberus, as dwellers of that realm.

She appears in a Minoan icon in her original Bronze Age context. One end-panel of the famous Hagia Triada sarcophagus (c. 1300 B.C.) supplies the context (Figure 17). This painted limestone sarcophagus probably once contained the body of a sacred king of Phaistos in Crete. It is generally agreed that the longer panels of this piece depict a funeral ceremony.[9] But the end-panel in question deserves a closer inspection than it has generally been given. It pictures two female figures in a chariot drawn by two Griffins and confronting a dark-winged flying bird with a crescent-shaped crest. The two women, who look up with a startled expression at the sudden appearance of the bird, are priestesses bearing the dead king to the underworld. The Griffins, relatives of the Sphinx, are lion-bodied, winged, and plumed and signify that the sacred king met a ritual death at the end of his calendar-regulated reign. Their crests have four feathers to symbolize the four-year half-cycle and their wings have nine feathers for the ninth year in which the king must die. As I have explained previously, the Minoan kings were sacrificed at the seventh lunation following the end of an eight-year cycle and, hence, in the ninth year of their reign. The priestesses are startled because the dark and crested bird is an epiphany of the great goddess herself in her death aspect. She has come to receive the soul of the sacred king. It is difficult to identify the species of the bird with certainty, but it is probably Perdix, the hen partridge, who was accounted the mother of the sacred king, Talos, the Cretan mythical figure who at death was turned into a cock partridge by Athena. What is significant is that her crest, very clearly rendered by the painter, has the form of the last crescent phase of the moon. She is Hecate in her Bronze Age manifestation as dark-winged, crescent-plumed bird, a receiver of the souls of the dead and associated with her calendar beasts, the Griffins.

The Griffin motif was carried from Crete to Mycenae. An example may be seen on an engraved seal from the East-

FIGURE 17. End panel of Hagia Triada sarcophagus. Late Minoan IIIa. Two priestesses drawn in a chariot by two Griffins bearing the dead sacred king to the after-world. Above, a crescent-crowned partridge is an epiphany of the moon-goddess as Hecate. HM., Gallery XIV, Case 171. *Heraklion Museum.*

West Wall (c. 1450–1350 B.C.). (Figure 18) The seal pictures two opposed Griffins on either side of a pillar supporting a receptacle for libations. Beneath them is a theriomorphic figure with human legs and a horned animal's head and forelegs. It appears to be a goat-man. In any case, it is a variant on the archetype of the sacred king combined with his calendar beast, like the Minotaur of Crete. The Griffins, paired as on the Hagia Triada Sarcophagus, represent the festival at which his reign ends.

FIGURE 18. Seal stone from Mycenae. (c. 1450–1350 B.C.) Above, a pillar and two opposed Griffins. Below, a goat-man.

An ivory plaque from Mycenae of a later date (c. 1200 B.C.) illustrates the relatedness of the Griffin to the Sphinx. (Figure 19) It features two Sphinxes confronting each other, with their forelegs resting on a central pillar. The parallel with the two Griffins of the earlier seal is plain. Below them are horns of consecration, a well-known altar emblem derived from Minoan Crete. Their heads are plumed with stylized lilies, a flower sacred to the Cretan goddess. But what is most interesting, and likely to be overlooked by anyone not familiar with the Knossos calendar, is the consistent calendric symbolism in the details of the carving. Both Sphinxes wear crowns with twelve points for the twelve months of regular years. On the other hand, their wings display two rows of feathers, the inner row consisting of eleven feathers while the outer row has thirteen. The symbolism is plain. Because of the eleven-day discrepancy between lunar and solar years, an irregular thirteen month year occurs three times in an eight-year cycle. This, too, is signified emblematically, for the Sphinxes have three locks of hair for the three intercalations. Their necklaces represent the cycle itself, since they have eight beads for the eight years of the full cycle and four pendants for the four years of the half-cycle. Finally, the symbolism is completed by a large spiral on their breasts and five small spirals on their wings. The five small spirals represent the five days of the winter solstice festival, which, as we have seen, are the special days outside the official year of 360 days, which belong to the calendar beast of the Griffin or Sphinx. The large spiral suggests the basic principle of the calendar—eternal return. Clearly the Bronze Age calendar of Mycenae was much like the Knossos calendar, if not identical.

Another Sphinx from Mycenae adds further evidence of such a calendar. Only the head of this Sphinx from the thir-

FIGURE 19. Ivory plaque from Mycenae. (c. 1200 B.C.) Two opposed Sphinxes with forelegs resting on a pillar.

teenth century B.C. is preserved (Figure 20). It is modeled lime plaster and painted. I have seen it in the National A chaeological Museum in Athens and I was struck by tl truly frightening effect it produces, with its large slantir eyes, downturned lips and ghastly white pallor. The effect achieves was no doubt intended, for the goddess, as Sphin is deadly. Her pale white face identifies her with the mooı What has not been previously recognized, so far as I aı aware, is that the artist has added deliberate calendric syn bolism to her features. Below a band which spans he forehead are crescent-shaped bangs of hair—five on he right-hand side in the shape of the old moon crescent and si on her left in the shape of the new moon crescent. Their oɾ position in the center of her forehead plainly indicates th same motif we have discovered in the riddle of the Sphin: previously discussed. "Who are the two sisters who give birtl to one another?" Certainly not "day" and "night." Th Sphinx herself tells us that the correct answer is the nev moon and the old moon or Artemis-Hecate. The birth take place at the full moon, graphically represented in the middlє of her forehead. The Sphinx herself is "Hecate at the cross roads" or the full moon, as her frightening full-face image asserts.

But why are there six crescents on one side and only fivє on the other? Because the artist was careless about sym- metry? No. Because six and five equals eleven, the calendaɾ secret of the number of days discrepancy between lunar and solar years. Now let us look at the strange symbols on both her cheeks and her chin. On her right cheek is a disk sur- rounded by exactly eight dots while her left cheek displays a similar disk also surrounded by eight dots, and a third disk on her chin is surrounded by nine. The calendric formula is obvious—a disk for the sun and eight dots for the solar-lunar cycle of eight years and nine dots for the ninth year at full moon of the seventh lunation, when the sacred king dies.

It is pertinent that we have on the authority of Lucian, Strabo, and Polybius the report that Atreus, king of Mycerae and father of Agamemnon and Menelaus of Homeric fame, was an astronomer.[10] If Homer may be trusted, Atreus should have been king of Mycenae about the end of the thir- teenth century and, hence, approximately contemporary with

FIGURE 20. Lime plaster head of Sphinx from Mycenae (thirteenth century B.C.) *National Archaeological Museum, Athens.*

the Sphinx examined above. The sacred kings of Mycenae of this period certainly knew the secrets of the eight-year solar-lunar calendar and, hence, had valid knowledge of astronomy. Another tradition recorded by Hyginus and Servius claims that Atreus was the first astronomer to predict an eclipse of the sun by mathematical means. His calculation proved correct and we are told that he won exclusive right to the throne from his brother and co-king, Thyestes, by virtue of his success.[11]

As I have shown in *The Thread of Ariadne,* the Knossos calendar together with a symbolic table of offerings from Phaistos indicate that the Minoans knew of the eclipse cycle known as the *saros* as early as the sixteenth century B.C. This cycle of eighteen years and 11 1/3 days may also have been known at Mycenae in the time of Atreus. If so, by this means Atreus might have predicted an eclipse.

Perseus, who in myth was held to be the founder of Mycenae, is closely connected with another relative of the Sphinx, the Gorgon, Medusa. The cluster of mythic tales that surround the figure of Perseus have come from various sources and consequently do not make up a consistent whole. With much of this we need not be concerned, but the episode of Perseus slaying Medusa has calendric significance and invites our attention.

According to mythic chronology, the dynasty founded by Perseus at Mycenae precedes by a considerable period of time the Pelopid dynasty begun by Atreus and his brother, Thyestes. It is probable, therefore, that the myth of Perseus and Medusa was derived from sources closer to the sixteenth than to the thirteenth century B.C.

The essential story is that Perseus set out to procure the head of Medusa with the help of Athena and Hermes. Athena gave him a mirror-like shield and warned him not to look at the Gorgon directly because her terrifying face turned men to stone. Hermes gave him a sickle as a weapon and helped him procure from the Stygian Nymphs a pair of winged sandals, a bag to contain the head safely, and a helmet which would make him invisible. So equipped, Perseus flew westward to the Land of the Hyperboreans, where he found Medusa and her two Gorgon sisters asleep among rain-worn shapes of men and beasts which had been turned

57

to stone. Looking into his shield at the reflection of Medusa, he cut off her head with the sickle; whereupon a surprising miracle ensued. From her severed neck emerged the winged horse, Pegasus, and a human twin, the warrior Chrysaor. He then secured the Gorgon's head in his bag and flew off southward to the realm of the Titan, Atlas, escaping the pursuit of the other two Gorgons by virtue of his helmet of invisibility.[12]

Before attempting to interpret this myth, it will be helpful to examine pertinent iconography and the family tree, as myth reports it, from which Medusa and her relatives derive. The descendants of Phorcys, a boar-king, and Ceto, a sea-goddess, may be seen in the chart in Figure 21.

The brood of Phorcys and Ceto were Ladon, a serpent who guarded the apples of immortality, Echidne, who was a woman from the waist up and a serpent below, and the three Gorgons, including Medusa. Echidne, in turn, bore to Typhon the three-headed dog, Cerberus, the hound of Hecate, and another two-headed dog, Orthrus. The dog Orthrus fathered on his own mother, Echidne, both the Sphinx and the Chimera. Medusa, as we have seen, gave miraculous birth to Pegasus, the winged horse, and Chrysaor. Chrysaor became the father of a three-bodied monster called Geryon, who kept the hound, Orthrus.[13]

From this chart alone, it becomes apparent that Medusa's relatives include a number of calendar beasts of the general type of the Sphinx with whom we began. Icons representing Medusa are many and varied and they help to reveal her calendric significance. While Medusa is not tripartite like the Sphinx, she does appear in triad as the three Gorgons. The three sisters here represent the three seasons. She parallels the Sphinx in being a frightening monster. Usually she is represented with snakes for hair, boar-like tusks (two crescents again), and a protruding tongue. Sometimes she is winged and frequently her legs are disposed in such a way as to suggest a triskelion or spinning moon-wheel.

The Gorgon's head as the center of a triskelion with three revolving winged feet may be seen on a Roman coin struck in 20 B.C. (Figure 22) But the motif is much older

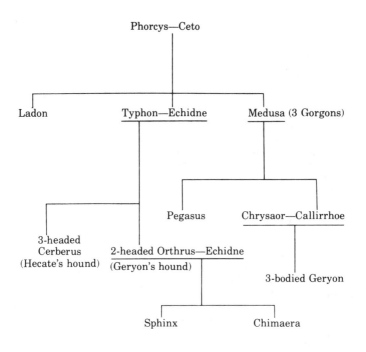

FIGURE 21.

than this example. At the Museum of Olympia, there is a
bronze fitting for a shield that dates c. 600–550 B.C. which
has the Gorgon's head in the center and three revolving
wings (Figure 23). One of the wings is now missing, but
there can be no doubt that there were originally three in all.
The original reference to the three legs or wings was to the
three phases of the moon—new, full, and old—as we have
observed in relation to Hecate. Medusa, again like the
Sphinx, represents a moon goddess.

Many full-length representations of Medusa show her
full-faced, but with her legs as if in motion sideways and

FIGURE 22. Roman coin of 20 B.C. Gorgon's head as the center of three revolving legs or a triskelion.

with knees bent (Figure 24). So far as I am aware, the reason for this peculiar position has never been explained. Surely its significance is as an echo of the triskelion motif—the moon-goddess in circular motion.

I have discovered two icons which relate Medusa directly with the Sphinx. One is a Laconian goblet in the Villa Giulia Museum in Rome, dating from the second half of the sixth century B.C. (Figure 25) The museum catalog describes the icon appearing on it as a God of the Winds chasing Harpies.[14] But the central position of the Sphinx in this icon would be meaningless in that context. It seems more likely that the male figure on the left with winged sandals, a sword, and a hand grasping the female figure's neck is Perseus. The winged female figure is not two Harpies, but a single creature with two heads. This is evident from the fact that there are only two wings, two legs, and two arms shown. This is a double-headed Medusa. In one hand she holds a small libation vase. Her other hand, raised in her own defense, has dropped a vessel with a tripod base and a snake emerging from its mouth. This is a sacred snake and the libation was being poured to it before the rude interruption of Perseus. The two-headed Medusa is a variation on the motif of the two heads, that of Chrysaor and Pegasus, emerging from her severed neck as in the Etruscan scarab illustrated in Figure 26. The presence of the Sphinx implies that in essence Medusa and the Sphinx are interchangeable symbols.

Another icon makes the identity of Medusa and the Sphinx unmistakable. It appears on a small vase from Nola and it portrays the Perseus myth in two panels (Figure 27). The first panel shows Hermes with his caduceus leading Perseus, who carries a sack and a sickle, toward a female figure robed in an ankle-length gown. Both wear winged sandals. The female figure stands before three sets of large shoul-

60

Figure 23. Bronze fitting for a shield. (c. 600–550 b.c.) Gorgon's head as center of winged triskelion. *Museum of Olympia.*

FIGURE 24. Sculpture from east pediment of the Temple of Artemis at Corcyra. (early sixth century B.C.) The Gorgon Medusa with arms and legs disposed to suggest revolving. On the right, her son, Chrysaor. *Museum of Corfu*.

der-wings which could be worn as ceremonial garb. She holds a spear and her neck is encircled by a serpent with nine heads. The second panel shows what has been assumed to be Medusa winged and decapitated with the infant Chrysaor beside her while Pegasus flies above. Fleeing from the scene are two identical winged male figures holding sickles aloft, as if to display their crescent-moon shapes. Behind Medusa

FIGURE 25. Laconian goblet. (sixth century B.C.) Perseus attacking a double-headed Medusa. Below a Sphinx. *Villa Giulia Museum, Rome.*

FIGURE 26. Etruscan scarab. Medusa with heads of Chrysaor and Pegasus emerging from her severed neck. Her arms and legs are disposed radially to suggest circular motion.

FIGURE 27. Two panels of a vase from Nola. Above, Hermes conducts Perseus to a priestess of the goddess, who will provide them and the sacred king with shoulder wings as regalia for a ritual regicide. Below, Perseus and Hermes, wearing shoulder wings, depart from the decapitated sacred king, who also wears a set of wings. Beside him at the right is the newborn sun-king, Chrysaor, while his soul as winged Pegasus ascends. On the pillar at right, the Sphinx presides over the entire ritual.

is a tall pillar with the Sphinx on the capital.

This is all so different from the literary myth that we could make nothing of it at all if it were not for the presence of the Sphinx. But we know the Sphinx to be a symbol of a particular calendar festival which falls at the end of a great year, and which involves a ritual regicide and the commencement of the reign of a new sacred king.

In this light the icons become intelligible. In the first panel, we find that the female figure's neck is encircled by a nine-headed serpent. This means that the ritual takes place at full moon of the seventh lunation following the end of the eight year cycle—in the ninth year of the king's reign. Who is this female figure? She is not the traditional ugly Gorgon, Medusa, although the snakes of Medusa encircle her head. Her spear is a traditional attribute of Athena and Athena was originally a Pelasgian goddess, whose son and consort was a serpent. The answer is that she is neither Athena nor Medusa, but a priestess whose ritual function is to represent both. The Pelasgian Athena was a fertility goddess in whose name the sacred king was ritually slain, and her priestesses wore Gorgon masks to represent her in her death aspect as Medusa at this particular calendar festival. Hermes, whose caduceus has two serpents of similar significance to hers, is conducting Perseus to the representative of the goddess, who will equip them and the sacred king with the shoulder-wings as regalia worn in the ritual sacrifice. I use "regalia" here in its original sense, meaning the "regal" emblem of kingship.

The sickle which Perseus carries is held with the hooked blade pointing down. This symbolizes the old moon crescent and contrasts intentionally with the upheld sickles representing the new moon in the second panel. The decapitation takes place at a time between that represented in the two panels, or, in other words, at full moon. The sack which Perseus carries was not originally intended as a receptacle for the head of Medusa. This is evident from the fact that in the second panel the two departing figures have neither sack nor head, but only upraised moon-sickles. The sack was originally a symbolic aspect of the ritual, like the basket carried in the Dionysus ritual at Eleusis. It stood for the womb of the great goddess from which the new-year babe would be born.

If we turn to the second panel, we find this interpretation borne out, for there is Chrysaor, the newborn king. The two receding figures now wear shoulder-wings, while the third pair of wings is worn by the decapitated figure from whose severed neck Chrysaor and Pegasus have emerged. The two departing figures no longer wear sandal-wings and they conspicuously hold their sickles aloft to signify the new moon crescent. The decapitated figure is not Medusa at all, much less the priestess of the other panel. This figure is masculine for he wears a short tunic with the hem above the knees of the same sort worn by the two departing figures, and his regal wings are identical with theirs. He is, in fact, the sacred king whom Perseus has ritually slain in Athena-Medusa's name.

In short, we see here a version of the twin king archetype. Perseus, whose name in Greek means "the destroyer," is the twin who slays his rival at the end of a great year cycle. They are solar-lunar calendar twins, the sickle signifying their lunar aspect while the wings represent their solar aspect. Hermes accompanies Perseus because he is the conductor of souls to Hades. But he is here for another reason as well. Wearing identical wings with the twins, Hermes represents the archetype of the transcendent third. The sacrificed sacred king dies a physical death, but his soul escapes to be reborn. This third aspect of a sacred king is a celestial one, here represented in another way by the immortal winged horse, Pegasus, who as the soul of the dying king emerges from the body and flies heavenward. The horse is in this case the king's totem beast, also reflected, as we have seen, in the mare's head of Hecate, the moon-mare being the mate of the sun-stallion. The new physically reborn king is Chrysaor, whose physical rebirth coincides with the soul's spiritual rebirth. This clearly explains the original significance of the icon of Pegasus and Chrysaor emerging from the severed neck, not the neck of Medusa, which makes no sense, but the neck of the dying sacred king as in this icon. It only remains to add that Chrysaor means "golden falchion" or "golden sickle," an appropriate name for a solar-lunar king, since the gold recalls the sun and the sickle the moon. And over all of this, the Sphinx on her pedestal presides.

Now if we return to the literary myth, we can see that it is the result of patriarchal misinterpretation or deliberate distortion of an older matriarchal ritual. The patriarchal Hellenes, perhaps the sixteenth-century dynasty of Perseus at Mycenae, modified the older religion. They made Perseus with the help of Hermes and Athena the champions of patriarchalism, and substituted for, or confused with, the slaying of a sacred king, the beheading of Medusa, the representative of the great goddess. Athena was herself originally this great goddess and Medusa was her death aspect and calendar emblem like the Sphinx. Her snakes and Medusa's snakes were the same, being male fertility symbols with a seasonal reference, as with the Minoan snake goddess. The Hellenes demoted Hermes to a messenger and converted Athena to the Olympian religion, saying that Zeus swallowed her real mother, Metis, who was already with child, and then gave birth to her from his forehead. They also said that Perseus presented her with the Gorgon's head, which she thereafter displayed on her shield as the Aegis. But that is a later twist to the story, for the Gorgon's head was hers from the first as the mask of her priestess, Medusa. A similar transformation of a matriarchal ritual into a hero's exploit can be seen in the myth of Bellerophon, who with the help of Pegasus, slew another relative of the Sphinx, the Chimera.

The well-known story of the power of the Gorgon's head to turn men to stone may be an echo of the stone pillar shrines of sacrificed sacred kings, the two pillars of which did originally represent the twin kings, while the central baetylic pillar represented his third transcendent aspect. Since Perseus was said to have slain Medusa among such dolmens in the western land of the Hyperboreans beyond the pillars of Hercules, it is conceivable that this story may have arisen from the memory of a Mycenaean visit to the dolmens of Stonehenge.

It should now be apparent how the Knossos calendar in conjunction with its related archetypes has made it possible to solve not merely one, but several of the riddles posed by the inscrutable Sphinx.

CHAPTER IV

Gemini

When Jason and the Argonauts sailed into the Sea of Marmara on their way to the Black Sea and the Golden Fleece, they landed on the island of Bebrycos to replenish their supply of water. Carrying their empty *amphorae,* the Argonauts approached a spring flowing with abundant fresh water, but Amycus, who ruled there as king, intercepted them and barred their way. This Amycus, a son of Poseidon, always refused hospitality to strangers unless they first met him in a boxing match. If they refused, he had them thrown over a cliff into the sea. When Amycus challenged the Argonauts, Polydeuces, who was an Olympic champion boxer, stepped forward and accepted. Polydeuces and his twin, Castor, were known as the Dioscuri or "divine youths" because Zeus was the father of the former, although not the latter, by the same mother.

After binding their hands and wrists with raw-hide thongs, they began to spar. Amycus was the heavier man, broad and brawny and very strong, but Polydeuces was as quick as a cat on his feet and a better boxer. He avoided the powerful but wild swings of Amycus until he had tired him, and then moved in with well-placed blows and finished him off. In fact, a final blow to the temple cracked his skull and he fell to the ground quite dead.

The Bebrycans, angered by the defeat of their king, attacked the Argonauts fiercely, but were repulsed and finally so badly beaten that Jason and his companions were able to sack the royal palace. They were able, then, not only to fill their jars with fresh water, but also to take aboard a stock of food and much booty. Jason then sacrificed twenty bulls to placate Poseidon and the Argonauts set sail. This is the substance of the legendary adventure as reported by the mythographers.[1]

There is little in this tale, which is merely a minor incident in the adventures of the Argonauts, that appears to have had a ritual origin, at least, if it be taken at face value. But when we recall that Castor and Polydeuces were twin princes of Sparta, that their mother was Leda, their twin sisters, Clytemnestra and Helen of Troy, and that Zeus was reputed the father of both Polydeuces and Helen, we begin to see that their twinship has roots in a prehistoric context.

We might also wonder why Amycus customarily had strangers thrown off a cliff into the sea if they would not box with him, if we were not aware that sacred kings of the prehistoric period sometimes escaped being ritually sacrificed at the end of a year or great year by substituting a captive as a surrogate victim. There is also evidence in both myth and icon that the victim or *pharmacos* was sometimes sacrificed in this particular manner, by being hurled into the sea from a height.[2]

In view of the ritual contests in which twin kings of the year engaged, the boxing of Polydeuces with the king of the Bebrycans looks suspiciously like a saga adventure derived from a ritual practice, the significance of which had been forgotten. That boxing matches were part of festival rituals among the Minoans has already been pointed out. Fresh light has been thrown on this practice by a very recent discovery on the island of Thera. Excavations on Thera (now Santorini) by Spyridon Marinatos are in the process of uncovering a Minoan city buried by the eruption of Thera's volcano in c. 1520–1500 B.C. A large part of the island itself exploded and the city was so rapidly buried in volcanic ash that the finds reveal an instant of living prehistory, like a fly preserved in amber. It is much like a Minoan Pompeii.

A most interesting find was a fresco depicting two young princes stripped down for action and engaged in a boxing match (Figure 28). They have long dark tresses and tight belts like Minoan bull-vaulters and they wear, apparently on one hand only, what I conjecture are probably ceremonial boxing gloves. The gloves are worn on the right hand only. But most interesting is the fact that their long black hair streams through blue headdresses. Professor Marinatos points out that this identifies them as royal princes, since Homer mentions characters with blue hair, an attribute of royalty of Eastern derivation that appears to have been also traditional among the Minoans of Thera.[3]

The two princes in the fresco are obviously of the same age and look enough alike to be twins. The one on the left wears a blue necklace of beads and a blue-beaded arm bracelet. These are probably also tokens of royalty since the priest-king relief fresco from Knossos pictures the young prince wearing a similar necklace. It is likely, then, that the fresco depicts not a casual boxing match, but a ritual contest between royal twins at a festival of the year, in symbolic reference to the archetype of the twin kings.

Let us return now to another boxing twin, Polydeuces of the royal house of Sparta. In the Villa Giulia Museum in Rome is a large, bronze cylindrical caldron known as the Ficoroni *Cista*. It dates from the fourth century B.C. and was found at Praeneste (Palestrina), a city in Latium which had Etruscan affiliations, and where a great many other *cistae* of this type were recovered from tombs. It is of particular interest, not only because it is the finest specimen of these *cistae*, but also because it features as a central motif the boxing match between Polydeuces and Amycus.

The body of the *cista* displays a scene depicting the moment immediately following the victory of Polydeuces over Amycus (Figure 29). Amycus, still wearing his raw-hide boxer's thongs, is being tied to a tree by Polydeuces, whose fists are also still bound with raw-hide. Above, a small winged Victory flies toward Polydeuces with a coronet and headband to crown the victor. To the right stands Athena, holding a lance and presiding over the entire scene. Observing this scene are two Argonauts on the right and two on the left, one of whom is winged. He is therefore either Zetes or Calais, one of another pair of mythic twins, the sons of Boreas, who were reputed to be winged, probably because Boreas, their father, was the North Wind.[4] At the base of the

70

FIGURE 28. Restored fresco of boxing boys from Thera. (c. 1500 B.C.)

tree to which Amycus is being tied lies a small child who is naked except for a loose garment wrapped about his shoulders. In his left hand, he holds a strigil, a spoon-like instrument used by athletes to scrape off the oil applied to their bodies before contests. In his right hand, he holds up a small pair of boots of open strap work. Tied to his left forearm by a strap is a small basket of a kind used by athletes to carry a strigil. However, it does not contain a strigil. On the contrary, three appendages of problematic significance may be clearly seen protruding from its wire work and hanging outside it. I shall return to this detail later. An axe lies conspicuously at the child's feet. Also, at the feet of Amycus, are a large pair of boots or buskins which have apparently been taken from him since he appears barefoot.

I have examined this *cista* and its engraved work in the Villa Giulia Museum with care, in order to avoid overlooking possibly significant details and to arrive at an accurate identification of everything the artist felt it was necessary to represent. It is obvious that a number of significant features

FIGURE 29 *(a)*. An engraved panel on the Ficoroni *Cista* from Praeneste. (Fourth Century B.C.) The victorious Polydeuces binds Amycus to a sacred tree in preparation for a ritual regicide, while Athena and the Argonauts attend. At the foot of the tree lies the intended victim, the child *Interrex. Villa Giulia Museum, Rome.*

FIGURE 29 *(b)*. Ficoroni *Cista*. Detail.

FIGURE 29 *(c)*. Ficoroni *Cista*. Lid and handle. Dionysus between two satyrs.

appear, which play no part in the saga incident as recorded in writing. But it is not difficult to account for them if we look away from the literary version, in the direction of the archetype of the twin kings and its associated context.

Amycus is a sacred fertility king, as attested by his buskins or sacred boots—the foot in the buskin being a phallic symbol later adapted to the protagonists of Greek tragedy. His boots have been removed because he has lost a ritual contest, upon the winning of which an extended term of his kingship depended. The child, who lies huddled at the foot of the tree, was to have been sacrificed as his surrogate. In such cases, the victim or *Interrex* was made king for a day, the day of the solstice, and then sacrificed. The child-sized sacred boots—identical in style to those of King Amycus—signify that he was to be sacrificed in place of the king. The sacrificial axe lies right beside them.

FIGURE 29 (d). Ficoroni *Cista*. Opposite side, showing Argonauts landing and a three-figure composition at foot.

However, the unexpected arrival of the Argonauts offered the alternative of an unknown stranger as *pharmacos*. The stranger would be forced to accept the challenge of Amycus, or suffer a ritual death by being thrown from a cliff. Amycus, who had defeated others in the past, was confident in his ability to out-box Polydeuces, in which case Polydeuces would have been the victim. But Polydeuces had been trained as a boxer, since a similar ritual obtained at Sparta. By winning the contest, Polydeuces will have also won the kingship, and Amycus will be sacrificed at the tree sacred to the great goddess, where the boy victim was to have been slain.

The presiding goddess in this scene is obviously Athena, since the emblem on her breast is the aegis. But she is a decidedly un-Greek Athena. With the exception of her lance, she lacks the war-like aspect of the Olympian Athena, daughter of Zeus. She wears no helmet and carries no shield. On the contrary her dress and pose are very feminine. Her hair is dressed in the manner of Etruscan ladies of fashion and she wears two necklaces and drop earrings. Her dress is thin, with buttoned sleeves and set off by a graceful cloak. But a symbolic note is struck by the appearance of three entwined snakes worn like a garland over her right shoulder, and she stands demurely with her right hand on her hip, displaying a snake bracelet on her dainty wrist.

The Etruscan goddess is really Minerva, who may only partially be equated with the Olympian Athena. She is closer to the Pelasgian Athena of prehistoric Athens, who was a fertility goddess joined in a sacred marriage with the reigning king as sun-serpent. The snakes draped over her shoulder and the snake bracelet are echoes of the Minoan fertility goddess, whose image was rendered with bare breasts and live snakes coiled about her arms.

Viewed in this light, it is not surprising that she presides over the boxing match of Amycus and Polydeuces. Apparently the scene takes place at the New Year when the twin kings must fight and the loser must suffer a sacrificial death tied to the sacred tree of the goddess, who in this case happens to be an Etruscan Minerva. That this is *her* sacred tree and not just any handy trunk is attested by the fact that it has twelve leafless and stylized boughs, representing the twelve months of the dying old year, and three leaf-bearing twigs, representing the three seasons of the new year to come.

Now let us return to the strigil basket tied to the left arm of the child at the base of the sacred tree. Certainly this detail must be meaningful, since the other objects about his person are symbolic. The axe is needed as a sacrificial weapon and the sacred boots serve to identify him as an *Interrex*. But if he is to be sacrificed, what need will he have for a strigil basket? The answer is that the basket is symbolic of the womb from which he will be reborn. The strigil itself is phallic in significance. This may be inferred by the fact that the basket does not contain a strigil, but three appendages which are very plainly phallic and meant to be equated with the strigil. The phallic symbolism of this death and rebirth ritual is emphasized again by the fact that both Amycus and Polydeuces have a short string tied about their penises.

Other motifs decorating the *cista* are consistent with the calendric and ritual significance of the boxing match of Amycus and Polydeuces. The upper border framing the boxing scene is made up of a series of Medusa heads, while the lower border features a series of Sphinxes in doublet facing each other with one paw raised. The lid of the *cista* shows in its central circle two lions facing two Griffins, with a young bull calf's head between one pair. All of these may be recognized as related calendar beasts signifying the New Year ritual.

The handle of the lid consists of Dionysus between two ithyphallic satyrs. The two satyrs represent the twin king archetype while here, Dionysus, a god who dies and is reborn, represents the transcendent third. The feet of the *cista* repeat this archetype in a variant form. They show a triad of male figures with the central figure standing while the twin figures sit. But, here, different figures play the archetypal roles. The right-hand twin is Hercules, identifiable by his traditional lion skin and club. I venture to identify the left-hand twin as Dionysus because he wears a panther skin and carries a staff which is probably the thyrsus—both traditional attributes of Dionysus. The central figure, the transcendent third, who appears to be holding up a strigil, is probably Hermes. As I shall show in the following chapter, it is Hermes who is usually found in the role of the transcendent third, although Dionysus sometimes assimilated the role of Hermes.

A further proof of the validity of the ritual and calendric intrepretation given to the Amycus and Polydeuces boxing match is provided by an engraved mirror, also from Praeneste, which may be seen in the same case in the Villa Giulia with the Ficoroni *Cista*. (No. 24864) The mirror features the same mythic subject, but treated with some revealing differences. It shows Amycus, with his hands taped for boxing, seated, while Polydeuces, also with hands taped, stands nearby. At the right is a sacred pillar which recalls the sacred tree in the *cista* scene. In the background between the contestants is a goddess wearing a mantle and himation and carrying a spear. She is placed so that she directly faces a crescent moon. In contrast, each of the boxers are represented by a four-rayed sun disk in the background. Both Polydeuces and Amycus have baskets on their arms, and are identified by their names in Etruscan: "AMUCES" and "POLOCES." The goddess is also identified in Etruscan as "LOSNA."

The iconography of this mirror reveals the ritual significance of the Amycus and Polydeuces myth very plainly. The two kings are shown to be sun-kings of the year by the two sun disks in the background, and the crescent moon by the goddess tells us that their contest was a ritual of the New Year regulated by a solar-lunar calendar. Like the boy in the *cista* scene, both of the sacred kings carry a basket, as a symbol of the womb and rebirth.

It is not difficult to see that the Etruscan name "AMUCES" is Amycus and that "POLOCES" is Polydeuces, who in Latin was called Pollux. But who is "LOSNA?" This puzzled me for some time, until by chance I came upon a number of engraved Etruscan mirrors in the Archaeological Museum of Florence, which depicted the Dioscuri in context with a female figure labeled in Etruscan "LASA." In several instances, "LASA" is winged and on one mirror she has feathers growing from her arms like wings, and she embraces a swan. Unquestionably the Etruscan "LASA" is equivalent to the Greek Leda, who was courted by Zeus in

78

the form of a swan and gave birth to the Dioscuri, the twins, Castor and Polydeuces, who emerged from a swan's egg. Therefore, "LOSNA" appearing in conjunction with Polydeuces and Amycus in a twin king icon, is probably a dialectical variant of "LASA" and equivalent to Leda, mother of Polydeuces. This implies that the Greek Leda was originally a moon-goddess whose sacred bird was the swan. Leda is just one more of the many names applied in different localities to the great goddess of the Bronze Age, who was invariably a moon-goddess wedded to a sun-king. The many extramarital affairs of Zeus, recorded in Greek mythology, reflect the absorption of the old matriarchal goddesses of the Bronze Age by the single patriarchal religion of Olympianism of which Zeus was the father-god.

I should like to point out one more example of the basket used as a symbol of the womb in Etruscan ritual. It appears in an account recorded by Clement of Alexandria, one of the early Christian church fathers. Clement describes a pagan cult of great antiquity in the vicinity of Mount Olympus in Macedonia. This was the cult of the Corybantes, whom, he says, were also called Cabeiri.

There were three brothers, two of whom slew the third, Corybas, wrapped his head in a crimson cloak, decked it with a wreath, carried it on a bronze shield to the foot of Mount Olympus and buried it. Thereafter, young men who were initiated in the cult were known as Corybantes after Corybas, and they were also called *Anaktotelestai* or "Initiates of the Kings." The two brothers of Corybas or Cabeiros took up a basket containing the phallus of the dead Dionysus and brought it to Etruria, where they lived in exile and taught the Etruscans to worship the basket and its contents.[5]

It is evident from this account that the head of Corybas-Cabeiros has been equated with the member of Dionysus, and that it symbolizes the fertility of a sacred king who has been ritually slain by his two brothers, the twin kings of the year. The slain brother is the transcendent third, the archetypal trinity discussed in relation to the Perseus myth. The young men initiates, it should be noted, are called initiates of the "Kings," (plural) and are, therefore, a variant of the archetype of the attendants on the kings. The basket containing a phallus is an unmistakable symbol of

79

impregnation of the womb and, hence, rebirth. We are told that the Etruscans in particular were aware of this significance. Furthermore, the boxing match of Amycus and Polydeuces took place on the island of Bebrycos, which is not far from Macedonia nor from the islands of Lemnos and Samothrace, where Jason's Argonauts, we are told, were initiated in the mysteries of the Cabeiri.[6] The connection of the Etruscans themselves with this general area is supported by a stone tablet inscribed with Etruscan letters dated about 600 B.C., which was discovered on the island of Lemnos.[7] We may, therefore, be reasonably sure that the basket held by the child on the Ficoroni *Cista* is a token of rebirth from the womb of the great goddess.

In discussing the myth of Perseus, twin pillar shrines or tombs, having reference to the twin kings, were briefly alluded to. This is an important variation on the twin-king archetype which deserves examination. Let us look at a Late Minoan Age example of this motif. It is a seal from east Crete (A.M. 1938.984) and was worn as a talisman, and therefore we may be sure that it had religious significance. (Figure 30) It features a rustic shrine with two wooden pillars supporting a pediment. Within is a large egg pierced by a phallic member, and two serpents parallel the two pillars on either side. This is a shrine of the twin kings of the year, who are signified by the two solar-serpents and by the two pillars paralleling them. The pillars are literally two trees, as may be seen from the forked branch on the right-hand one. In addition to being represented by totem beasts, the twin kings were also represented by sacred trees. We have already seen that the fertility bough was frequently an attribute of sacred kings. The oak club of Hercules and the laurel of Apollo are echoes of this very ancient tradition.

But what is the meaning of the pierced egg within the shrine? When we recall that the twin kings annually die and are reborn as sons of the goddess, the answer becomes plain. This is not only a shrine; it is also a tomb. In death the twin kings return to the womb of the mother-goddess, where the male and female principles are united and from which they are reborn. The phallic member piercing the egg is the symbol of this union after death. The swan's egg of Leda, whom Zeus consorted with as a swan, is, as we have seen, a later

> Oak symbolising the oak's
Strength of Herculese.

FIGURE 30. Late Minoan Talismanic gem from East Crete. (AM. 1938.984) Two serpents surmounting rustic shrine of two pillars with pierced egg within. *Ashmolean Museum.*

example of this symbol. The proof of this equation is that from the egg of Leda the Dioscuri, Castor and Polydeuces, were born. And in classical iconography, these Spartan twins are frequently pictured with conical caps resembling the two halves of Leda's egg.

The specifically calendric significance of this motif lies in the analogy of the two pillars of the shrine upholding a lintel with a threshold below, and the Knossos fresco with its two vertical columns and the equivalent of a lintel above and a threshold below—the two horizontal beams. And this is verified by the fact that the two halves of serpent season, when the sun dies at the midpoint (winter solstice), are represented on the calendar by precisely these two vertical columns or pillars. No wonder the two serpents are represented on the seal as parallel to the two pillars.

A further variation on this motif also had its origin in Minoan times. Another talismanic gem from Crete (A.M. 1938.997) of the late Minoan Age illustrates this (Figure 31). It features two beaked ewers, disposed antithetically like the two pillars on the shrine discussed above. The handles are long and serpentine in shape, recalling the serpents parallel to the pillars in the previous example. Between the vessels is a stylized tree of life. The two vessels are symbolic of burial urns for the twin kings and the serpentine handles recall their solar-serpent aspect. Consequently this seal also signifies a tomb of the kings. Instead of a pierced egg as a central member, we find a tree of life representing the life giving mother-goddess. The central member of this motif in Minoan art has many variations—an egg, a tree, a baetylic pillar, an *omphalos,* a double axe, a labyrinth design—but all

81

represent without contradiction the womb of the mother-god-dess, as well as the union of the male and female principles and, hence, rebirth.

FIGURE 31. Late Minoan Age talis-manic gem from Crete. (AM. 1938.997) Two beaked ewers with a stylized tree of life as the central member of a triad. *Ashmolean Museum.*

Now let us look at a Greek example of this motif dating from the Archaic Period. It is a stone relief from Sparta, where, as we have seen, the twin solar kings became the Dioscuri. (Figure 32) The relief is shaped like a twin pillar shrine with a border simulating uprights, supporting a lintel and pediment. Within, parallel to the pillars, are the Dios-curi, carrying lances and wearing the halved-egg caps as is their wont. Between them are two identical *amphorae* with lids, recalling the burial urns discussed above. In the pedi-ment is the egg of Leda, their mother, and it is flanked by two solar-serpents representing the death and rebirth of the sun at winter solstice.

A further example of this motif from late antiquity (c. second century B.C.) is provided by an interesting relief now in the Verona museum (Figure 33). It was a votive given by a certain Argenidas in honor of the Dioscuri after the donor had successfully completed a voyage, as the Greek inscrip-tion indicates. He was probably a Spartan who travelled to Venice, where the relief appears to have been carved. On the left are the Dioscuri in their egg-shaped caps. Before them is an altar with a relief of a boar on it, a frequent motif on Ital-ian altars of this period. Behind it is a platform upon which rests two lidded *amphorae*. The bearded figure to the right, pouring a libation on the altar, is Argenidas.

FIGURE 32. Archaic relief from Sparta. The Dioscuri within a pillar shrine. Between them are two identical *amphorae*. Above, the swan's egg of their mother, Leda, between two solar-serpents.

Behind him on the right is his ship safely in a harbor overlooked by hills. To the right of the ship are two bull's heads, probably representing sacrifices made to the twins. Above the ship at the right top corner are two twin-pillared shrines, which .may be identified by the inscription below them as the *Anakeion* (sanctuary of the "Lords"), a double

83

FIGURE 33. Stone relief of the second century B.C. A votive given by Argenidas in honor of the Dioscuri. At left, the Dioscuri before two *amphorae* on an altar. At right, Argenidas pouring a libation. Behind him, his ship, two twin-pillar shrines with a cave beneath, from which a serpent emerges to accept the offering. *Verona Museum.*

shrine of the Dioscuri. It has beneath it an underground cave in which may be seen two figures lying down and three additional figures upright. On a stone of the cave at the far left is an image of a cock. From the sanctuary a snake crawls out, extending toward the *amphorae*.

The interpretation of the icon is not difficult. Argenidas, in gratitude for a safe voyage, is offering a libation to the twin kings (the "Lords"), his protectors. The two *amphorae* in this case do not contain the ashes of the twins, but the libation offering. The snake, representing the soul of the twins, emerges from their actual tomb, the cave beneath their sanctuary, and crawls to the *amphorae* to accept the offering. The sanctuary above the cave is simply a twin-pillared shrine, doubled. In Sparta this doubled type of twin-pillared shrine was known as the *dokana*, the *Anakeion* being merely a specific shrine of that type. The cave, which is a womb symbol, represents the goddess, and the two reclining figures within it are the twin kings. That the two kings are about to be reborn is symbolized by the cock, whose crowing at dawn awakens the sun-kings. Their raised hands show that they are awakening. The three remaining figures in the cave are Curetes, the attendants upon the sacred kings. They, together with the kings, make five in all, being in another sense, the five Dactyls (five "fingers" of the hand of the goddess). The Dactyls, as we have seen, are a variant on the Curetes or attendants on the kings. Thus we see that the ancient calendric origin of the twin king motif is still recognizable in an icon of the second century B.C.

Another significant variation on the twin king archetype represents each twin with one knee bent so that the heel of the foot does not come in contact with the earth. A number of Etruscan mirrors illustrate this motif, in relation to the Dioscuri. In every case the twins are equated with the two pillars of their traditional shrine, and they usually support a lintel of some kind—an architrave or pediment—and a symbolic third member, usually also pillar-shaped, is shown between them in the shrine.

One example pictures them upholding a lintel with their heads while the central member is a palm tree (Figure 34). The objects behind them are their shields. The important fact to note is that the twin on the left has his left heel raised and resting on his shield while the one on the right has his right heel raised and so rested. The palm tree within the shrine they form is a tree of life with the significance we have previously noted.

Another example is more naturalistically rendered (Figure 35). Here the twins, wearing their traditional eggshell caps, support an architrave under which we find an eight-rayed sun disk, and below that a swan. They are encircled by a garland composed of two sprays of double leaves—eight on each. Here again the left-hand twin raises his left heel, while the other raises his right heel. The swan obviously represents their mother, Leda, a moon-goddess and the eight-rayed sun is her sun-king mate. The garland emphasizes eight as the calendar cycle number.

In these examples, as well as in many other variants on this motif, the twins, like Oedipus, have a sacred heel which may not be allowed to come in contact with the earth. But

FIGURE 34. Engraved Etruscan mirror. The Dioscuri as pillars upholding a lintel. Each has an alternate heel resting on his shield to avoid contact with the earth. Between, a palm as tree of life.

FIGURE 35. Engraved Etruscan mirror. The Dioscuri with egg-shell caps supporting a lintel. Beneath the lintel is an eight-rayed sun and a swan.

why? I believe the explanation can be inferred from the fact that the twins, in every example of this motif I have seen, are shown with opposite heels raised. The earth, of course, may be equated with the mother-goddess who is joined with both twins in a sacred marriage. However, since one is king of the waxing year, his sacred union with her lasts only to the summer solstice when he dies and his twin replaces him, the king of the waning year. Since the twins are united with the earth-goddess in alternate halves of the year, this union is symbolized by an alternate foot of each in contact with the earth.

This also provides the clue to the mythic theme of the death of a hero, who is killed by receiving a wound in the heel. The vulnerable heel of Achilles is best known, but there are many other parallels such as Philoctetes and Cheiron, the centaur, both of whom were wounded in the heel by a poisoned arrow, and the Cretan Talos, who died from a pin stuck in his heel by Medea. The meaning of all these myths is basically the same. The sacred king or his tanist suffered death at the solstice by receiving an en-venomed arrow or bodkin in his "vulnerable heel," that is the particular heel, left or right, which was not in ritual practice allowed to come in contact with the life-giving force of mother earth. The raised heel was therefore vulnerable, just as the giant Antaeus, whose mother was the earth, could not be strangled by Hercules until he had lifted him from contact with the ground.

A final variation on the twin king archetype which has revealing significance may be seen on a number of coins from the island of Tenedos. Tenedos is an island close enough to the Troad to be seen from the mainland. A series of coins struck there from the sixth century B.C. onwards show a Janiform head consisting of a male and female profile combined on one side and a double axe on the obverse.[8] A specimen now in Berlin shows a feminine face on the left, joined with a masculine face on the right (Figure 36). The obverse shows a double axe above three steps and between twin pillars. The letters in the field identify the coin as one struck at Tenedos. Since the Janiform head with its opposed faces is analogous to the opposed faces of the double axe, it is apparent that they are, in a sense, equivalents.[9] We may recognize in the twin pillars the motif of the twin kings, and the double axe between them is a combination that appears in Minoan art. The axe appears as the central member of twin pillar shrines and also between bull's horns or horns of consecration. In fact, these latter combinations, as we have seen, gave rise to the labyrinth motif. And we have also seen

87

that it is in the labyrinth that the sacred kings are united after death with the goddess. The Janiform head, which is both male and female, must therefore represent the union of sun-king and moon-goddess in the afterlife. The double axe is an equivalent in meaning as well as in shape, because the axe blades as opposed crescents represents the moon-goddess, while the pillar-like shaft represents the male member united with her.

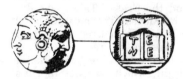

FIGURE 36. Coin from Tenedos. At left, a Janiform head composed of a male and female face. The obverse displays a double axe between twin pillars.

The joined male and female heads may be further understood by reference to the local legend about the founding of the kingdom of Tenedos. A king of the neighboring Troad called Cycnus, which means "swan," had a son by the name of Tenes by his first wife. After her death, Cycnus remarried and his second wife attempted without success to seduce her step-son, Tenes. Angered at the rebuff, she accused Tenes of attempting to violate her and Cycnus believed her. Thereupon Cycnus locked Tenes and his sister, Hemithea, in a chest and set them adrift on the sea. They were washed ashore on an island where Tenes founded a kingdom, and thereafter the island was called Tenedos after him. Later Cycnus discovered that he had been deceived, and, hearing of the whereabouts of Tenes, he sailed for Tenedos to seek forgiveness. But Tenes stubbornly refused to receive him, cutting the hawser of his father's moored ship himself with an axe. This gave rise to the proverbial expression for an angry refusal—"He cut him off with an axe from Tenedos."[10]

Archaeological finds on Tenedos indicate that the island had connections with Minoan Crete in the Bronze Age, so it is not inappropriate to look in that direction for an understanding of the myth, the double axe, and the bisexual Janiform head. Cycnus as a swan-king identifies him as a sacred king of the pre-Hellenic religion, reflected subsequently in the myth of the Greek Zeus making love to the pre-Hellenic goddess, Leda, in the guise of a swan. Cycnus' suspicion of his son's advances toward the queen, and his setting of Tenes and his sister adrift in a chest closely parallels the story of how Danaë and her son Perseus were set adrift in a chest by Acrisius because he feared that his grandson, Perseus, would kill him. In both tales, the king's fear would be a reflection of the fact that he held his kingship by virtue of his union with the queen and that he could be replaced by ritual regicide. Why Cycnus casts off his innocent daughter, Hemithea, as well as the suspected Tenes is left unexplained in the myth. But it probably reflects the fact that by matrilinear succession the queen's daughter's husband becomes king, not the king's own son, unless, like Oedipus, he marries his mother, or his stepmother, which was what Cycnus feared from Tenes. Cycnus' unmarried daughter is therefore also a threat to his reign.

The chest or ark adrift at sea carrying mother and child or brother and sister has many parallels in myth and folktale. It even appears in Chaucer's "Man of Law's Tale." Its fundamental significance is as a symbol of the union of the son with the mother in the womb or, in a more metaphysical sense, the union of the male and female principles in an androgynous state after death and before rebirth. Hemithea's name, literally translated, means "half-goddess," but the literal rendering is a trifle misleading. Hemithea is a "half-goddess" in the sense that she, in the chest with Tenes, is only one half of a unity which includes both the male and female principles. That is why her half-profile united with the half-profile of Tenes appears upon the Tenedos coins and is repeated by another symbol of that union, the double axe, on the obverse side. The axe makes its appearance in the myth in the sense of a sacrificial weapon. Tenes does not literally kill his father, Cycnus, but he cuts the hawser of his father's ship with the axe and therefore sets his father adrift in an ark on the sea. In short, he repays his father in kind!

The Janiform head, however, does not always have the significance explained above. More frequently, as in the Latin god, Janus, both faces are male. In this combination, the union usually signifies the twin kings of the year looking in opposite directions to suggest the bipartite year. Our month of January, named after Janus, is appropriately the first month of the year.

We have now explored the twin-king archetype in its calendric context. Sets of twins of fundamentally similar significance abound. There are, for instance, Herakles and Iphicles, Idas and Lynceus, Romulus and Remus, Cain and Abel, and Osiris and Set, to name but a few. The archetype and its related customs left a mark upon Western history and culture. The influence may be seen in the two consuls of the Roman Republic, the king for a day of carnival festivals, which reflects the *Interrex,* the modern cartoons of Old Father Time and his scythe giving way to the New Year Babe, and no doubt in other customs not suspected of such an origin. The archetype reaches back in time at least five thousand years and possibly more, for before Olympian Zeus set his twins in the sky as stars, the Minoans knew them as sun-twins, and even before that the Sumerians of Mesopotamia knew them as season-kings and as the twins, Gemini, which as a sign of the Zodiac, in their day, ushered in the spring equinox and their New Year.[11]

CHAPTER V

Thrice Great Hermes

The Linear B tablets discovered at Nestor's palace at Pylos record offerings made to various divinities. Many of these divinities of the thirteenth century Pylians can be recognized as antecedents of the classical gods of Olympus. Some, however, remain unidentified with classical counterparts. A number of them probably did not survive the Dark Ages following the Dorian invasion, but others may yet be identified. One styled *Trisheros* or the "Thrice-Hero" has remained, so far as I am aware, an unsolved mystery. Emily Vermeule in her *Greece in the Bronze Age* (1966) writes, "The Triple Hero is popular at Pylos, though he has no good classical counterpart; the name should mean Great Hero, Triply Great."[1] I believe it can be shown that *Trisheros* is an epithet for Hermes.

In chapters III and IV, I have already called attention to Hermes in the role of the archetype of the transcendent third. Detailed evidence for that identification is now in order as a preliminary to a discussion of the Mycenaean significance of the deity called *Trisheros.*

Hermes is the greatest enigma of all the twelve Olympian gods. Since myth tells us that he was a son of Zeus born out of wedlock to Maia, a daughter of Atlas, the Titan, in a cave on Mount Cyllene in Arcadia, it is evident that he was known to the non-Hellenic Pelasgians.[2] That Zeus consorted with Maia, a Pelasgian representative of the great goddess, simply reflects the absorption of a local Arcadian cult by the Olympian religion. The Titans, like the Dactyls, were not gods at all in the Olympian sense, but ritual attendants on a sacred king. The early Pelasgians would have recognized no actual divinity other than the all-embracing great goddess. The name Hermes means "pillar" and this identifies him as a being rather different from a god, namely, a hero. As we have seen, the twin kings of the year were represented by twin pillars supporting the lintel of a shrine-tomb, within which we usually find a third member, frequently a baetylic pillar. This central pillar is the "Herm" from which Hermes derives his name. The herm is an emblem of a "hero," a word which in its original sense meant "one beloved by Hera."

Let us look closely at some of the rather strange things that the mythological tradition records about Hermes. He is certainly a very paradoxical figure. First of all in sex. One of his titles was Hermes Tychon or Aphroditos Tychon.[3] As such he was a masculine Aphrodite or, more accurately, a bisexual figure. There is also the mythical account of his mating with Aphrodite. The offspring of this union was Hermaphroditus, again a figure neither male nor female but both. There appears to be a parallel here with Cretan Androgeus, whose name implies that he was androgynous or bisexual. Androgeus was the child of King Minos and Queen Pasiphaë of Knossos. And it is perhaps worth noting that Pasiphaë was said to be the mother of a child called Cydon by Hermes.[4] Hermes is also credited with having invented the fire-drill, a wooden spindle spun in a hole in a board, to produce a spark quickened by tinder. This primitive fire-making device suggested to the mythopoeic mind the union of the masculine and feminine principles. What is more, in Hermetic alchemical lore, much of which had very ancient sources, Hermes as "Mercurius" was a prime symbol in the search for the philosopher's stone, because it was thought to combine "sol" and "luna" or the sun and the moon and, hence, the male and female principles respectively.[5]

In another sense he is paradoxical because he is both a celestial and a chthonic god. He resides on Mount Olympus and flies swifter than the wind on winged sandals to the most distant parts of the upper world, yet he is also equally at home in the underworld of Hades, for he is the conductor of the souls of men to the depths of Tartarus.[6] One of his epithets is Hermes Chthonios or "Hermes of the Depths."[7] Nor are these depths merely physical, for another of his epithets is Hermes Psychopompos, which indicates that he could initiate one in the secrets of the soul, or what we would call today the depths of the unconscious.[8] And this is in keeping with his reputed oracular powers of augury and divining. He was also a god credited with mental subtlety and great ingenuity, for he helped the Three Fates in the composition of the alphabet, invented astronomy, the lyre, the musical scale, the arts of boxing and gymnastics, weights and measures, and the game of dice.[9]

The lyre which he invented, we are told by myth, had three strings and these were said to represent the three seasons. This is a clue worth noting since it associates him with both of the twins of the year, represented by the spring and summer seasons, and with the third season as well, the winter. Another clue to his original significance is the caduceus, which in both myth and icon is his ever-present emblem. The caduceus, now the symbol of the medical profession, is a golden staff entwined by two serpents, each curled two and one half turns about it. The caduceus is gold to suggest the sun-kings, and entwined by two serpents to represent the twin kings in serpent season, when one dies and is reborn as the other. The serpents are two and one-half turns about the staff to symbolize the five days of the winter solstice festival, two and one-half days sacred to each. But the staff itself is a shaft or pillar *between* the two serpents. It is the central member just as the baetylic herm is the central member in the icons of the twin pillar shrines. This central pillar is the emblem of Hermes, who is neither twin but the transcendent form of both.

In discussing the myth of Perseus, I have previously called attention to this transcendent form of the solar twins. It may now be seen why Hermes and his counterpart, Perseus, play major roles in that myth. Hermes together with the twins compose a trinity. That is why the baetylic pillar or herm stands within the twin pillar shrines or tombs. Both twins are "heroes," that is beloved of the goddess, but Hermes is the "Thrice-Hero" because he incorporates the two in a third.

We have also seen that iconography implies that in the transcendent state, the male and female principles are united. We may recall the Minoan seal illustrated in Figure 30 showing a central member of a twin pillar shrine, consisting of an egg pierced by a phallus. Hermes, then, as the central transcendent form of the twins unites the male and female principles. This explains the bisexual paradoxes recorded about him in mythology.

In this light it also becomes clear why Hermes is both a celestial and a chthonic god. Incarnate as the solar twins, he is of this world and courses the heavens, but he returns periodically to the womb of the earth-mother to be reborn. His original significance also explains why in the Olympian religion he was given the function of conducting the souls of the dead to the underworld. His paradoxical nature as the Thrice-Hero had been forgotten by Homer's time, but when he became an Olympian god, he retained his celestial character as a messenger and his chthonic relationship to the earth and the underworld as the conductor of souls to Hades.

An interesting icon identifying Hermes as the transcendent form of the twin kings may be seen on a coin from Volterra in Etruria dated c. 350 B.C. (Figure 37) The coin shows the twin kings as a Janiform head. The two heads are covered by a single pointed *petasos*, the hat of Hermes. That the *petasos*, usually shown on the head of Hermes, here covers both heads and unites them, implies that Hermes is a third member of this emblem and transcends the other two.

The opposite side of this coin shows a club and a new moon crescent encircled by Etruscan letters. The club signifies a sacred king, such as Hercules was, and the new moon would be a reference to the moon-goddess, his bride. By converting the Etruscan letters to their known equivalents in our alphabet, I get "VELATHRI." This is known to be the Etruscan name for the city which the Latin language approximated as Volterra, where the coin was struck.[10] The Janiform head under the *petasos* in context with a crescent moon and a club, suggests that this is probably an Etruscan emblem of *trisheros* or Hermes.

A *krater* from Ruvo, now at Naples, provides another icon of significance (Figure 38). It shows Hermes slaying Argos. According to myth, Zeus made love to Io and aroused

94

FIGURE 37. Etruscan coin from Volterra. At left, a Janiform head capped by the *petasos* of Hermes. The obverse exhibits a crescent moon and a club and the Etruscan inscription "VELATHRI." (c. 350 B.C.)

the jealousy of Hera. To protect Io, Zeus turned her into a white cow, but Hera claimed the cow as her own. She then set Argos Panoptes, a creature with a hundred eyes, as guard over the cow, Io, to make sure that Zeus would not touch her again. But Zeus sent Hermes to free Io. Hermes knew he could not avoid being seen from any angle by Argos' eyes. Therefore he did not attempt to free Io by any sleight of hand, but charmed Argos to sleep by playing the flute and then cut off his head and set Io free.[11]

That is the literary myth, but the icon tells a rather different story. It shows Hermes on the left grasping Argos by the arm and making ready to slay him with a sword. To the right of Argos is Io, who is pictured as a maiden with cow's horns. Argos is Janiform with one head bearded and the other beardless, and both heads are covered by the *petasos*. With his right hand he wields a club, and his left shoulder is draped in a panther skin. On his body he has nine eyes but the profiled heads show two more for a total of eleven eyes in all.

In the myth there is nothing whatever said about Argos having a hat, a panther skin, and a club, nor does he have a Janiform head. And he is supposed to have a hundred eyes,

FIGURE 38. A *krater* from Ruvo. Hermes at left is about to slay Argos. Argos has nine eyes on his body, a Janiform head covered by a *petasos,* a panther skin, and a club. Io at right has the horns of a cow.

not nine or eleven. The icon plainly records the tradition of an earlier Argos. The Janiform head recalls the twin sacred kings. One head is bearded to represent the dying old sun of the year at the solstice, while the other is beardless to signify the youthful sun of the New Year. The *petasos* unites them, just as on the coin from Volterra. The club, which also appears on the Volterra coin, is the club of Hercules, once a sacred king whose club was originally a fertility bough. The panther skin is the usual robe of Dionysus, who was a dying god derived also from the archetype of a sacred sun-king. The nine eyes on the body of Argos are sun symbols. The eye appears in numerous mythic contexts as a symbol of the all-seeing sun. One myth tells of the monster Typhon swallowing the eye of the Egyptian sun-god, Horus, and then restoring it, which was said to signify an eclipse of the sun.[12] The single eye of the Cyclops was originally also a sun-eye.[13] And a number of Minoan seal stones display an eye in a context which suggests that it represented the sun. The name Argos means "the bright one," which is also appropriate as an epithet for the sun.[14]

This Argos has nine eyes because the solar-lunar calendar calls for the death of the sacred king in the ninth year, eight and one-half years after the beginning of a cycle. If we consider the additional two eyes in the head as significant, the total becomes eleven which is the number of days of discrepancy between solar and lunar years. This Argos is obviously a solar king being slain at the end of his reign.

In that case, Io is not being freed from Argos. On the contrary, Argos is being sacrificially slain in her honor, for she is the moon-goddess. She is a white cow-goddess with horns like the crescent moon. As we have seen, the moon-goddess is often pictured as a lunar cow mated to a solar bull. The twin kings are in this case variants of Hercules and Dionysus, and since they wear the hat of Hermes, and Hermes slays them, the meaning is that Hermes, as their transcendent form, stands for death in life but also for life in death. Clearly Hermes is ultimately a mythic figure whose triple form represents the archetype of the transcendent third.

Although the orthodox mythographers of the classical period had lost sight of this archetypal Hermes, the Thrice-Hero, others, and particularly those concerned with secret and mystical doctrines, retained a memory of his original significance. That they did so is evident in the doctrine of the Gnostics. A curious mystical treatise from Alexandria in Egypt called the *Kyranides* appears under the name of one who calls himself, Hermes Trismegistus or "Thrice Great Hermes." The author claims in his preface to be combining materials from two older books. One of these he claims was the book of Kyranos, King of Persia, who lived at the time of King Solomon. The other was a book dedicated by Harpokration of Alexandria to his own daughter. The date of this compilation is unknown, but it was written at some time prior to c. 408 A.D.[15]

Internal evidence suggests that the various related mystical texts attributed to Hermes Trismegistus were probably the work of several hands, written at different times and collected and preserved by a school of Hermetic philosophers.[16]

These syncretists of Alexandria drew from many ancient sources, and, among them, the Egyptian God, Thoth, was generally equated with Hermes. Whatever their immediate sources may have been, their central doctrine contains elements reminiscent of the archetypal Hermes, "the Thrice-Hero," from whom they also derived their pseudonymn.

According to their doctrine, one can apprehend through mystic *gnosis* that the apparent dualities and oppositions of this world are transcended by a divine Third, which is both a Trinity and a Unity. This transcendent Three-in-One is the Godhead and is described as bisexual, incorporeal, immortal, and essentially circular in form. This mandala, perceived by the eye of the intellect rather than the senses, is said to be Life and Light and the source of man's soul. It is also the source of all creation, motion, and dissolution. To apprehend this mystery through *gnosis* is to be spiritually reborn.[17]

It is apparent that this metaphysical doctrine remarkably parallels the archetypal significance of Hermes, "the Thrice-Hero," that we have detected in myth and icon as underlying the classical Olympian God. "The Thrice-Hero" transcends the duality of the twins, is bisexual when in union with godhead, is luminous like the sun, and promises rebirth and immortality in a circle of eternal return. It is also interesting that the so-called Hermes Trismegistus alludes to what he calls "the hidden meaning of knife or double axe," but he does not tell us what the hidden meaning is.[18] We have already seen some of the connotations of the double axe and we shall explore the problem further in a later chapter. But let us look now at *Trisheros* as he appears in the Mycenaean context of the Pylos tablets.

Trisheros is a title which appears on two tablets from Pylos—on Fr 1204, where he is the recipient of an offering of oil, and on Tn 316, where he is the recipient of a votive offering of a gold cup.[19] The latter tablet is by far the most interesting, because it shows *Trisheros* in what is certainly a calendric context. This tablet is inscribed on both sides, which is a departure from the usual practice, and it appears to have been made to record a very special religious rite, one differing from the regular annual rites, since those routine rites are recorded elsewhere in a related series of tablets filed together; whereas this double inscribed tablet appears alone.[20]

Chadwick's revised translation (1973) of the two sides of this tablet is as follows:

REVERSE

In the month of Plowistos, Pylos
sacrifices at *Pa-ki-ja-ne* and
brings gifts and leads *victims.*
For the Mistress: one gold cup, one woman.
For *Mnasa:* one gold bowl, one woman.
For Posidaeia: one gold bowl, one woman.
For the *thrice-hero*: one gold cup.
For the *Lord of the House,* one gold cup.
Pylos . . . (blank)
OBVERSE
Pylos *sacrifices* at the shrine of Poseidon
and the *city* leads, and brings gifts
and leads *victims*: one goldcup,
two women, *for G w owia (and?)*
Komawenteia.
Pylos *sacrifices* at the shrines of *Perse*
and Iphemedia and Diwia, and
brings gifts and leads victims:
For *Perse*: one gold bowl, one woman.
For Iphemedeia: one gold bowl.
For Diwia: one gold bowl, one woman.
For Hermes *Areia*: one gold cup, one man.
Pylos *sacrifices* at the shrine of Zeus
and brings gifts and leads *victims:*
For Zeus, one gold bowl, one man.
For Hera, one gold bowl, one woman.
For *Drimios* the *son* of Zeus, one gold bowl (?)
Pylos . . . (blank)[21]

This is the way the entries look, but it must be added that both faces of this tablet are divided by cross-lines into five sections, and the fourth and fifth sections on each side have been deliberately left blank. "The only other tablet which shows similar blank entries," writes Chadwick, "is Knossos 207 = V 280, which is introduced by a month name and which there is reason to think represents a calendar or diary of fifteen successive days."[22] Similarly the five sections in which each side of this tablet is divided suggests very strikingly a record of the rites performed during the special five-day winter solstice or New Year Festival of the Knossos calendar. It could be interpreted to mean that certain rites and human sacrifices were performed at specific shrines on the first three days of the festival, while on the last two days no rites were performed but the days were holidays, being the remainder of the five-day festival.

There is a significant parallel between the entries on the obverse and the reverse in regard to *Trisheros* and Hermes. In rites carried out at two different shrines during the same festival, three feminine deities are honored in conjunction with one masculine deity, who in one case is called *Trisheros* and in the other, Hermes. It is reasonable to infer that both references are to a single deity, Hermes *Areia* (untranslated), whose epithet is *Trisheros*. At Knossos we find Poseidon called *Ennosigaion* or "Earth-Shaker" and Ares called *Enyalios* or "Battle God," both epithets, while they are called Poseidon and Ares on other tablets.[23] This substitution of epithet for proper name is common in Homer, and it is no surprise to find it earlier.

The offering of gold vessels and the sacrifice of human victims is not at all common at Pylos. The tablets show that ordinarily the offerings to the deities are gifts of wheat, olive oil, wine, honey, or spices. Therefore, it seems probable that this festival recorded on a single isolated tablet was not the regular New Year festival, but a very special festival at the end of a great year, the eight-year cycle of the solar-lunar calendar. The presence of Hermes would seem to support this conclusion, for, as we have seen, he is associated with both Perseus and Argos in the slaying of a sacred king. As *Trisheros* he would represent the transcendent third—the sacred king's transcendence of death after a ritual regicide. On the reverse of the tablet, Hermes as the *thrice-hero* appears together with a triad of goddesses, who apparently receive the human sacrifices as a surrogate for the sacred king. It is possible that the sacred king himself is here designated as "Lord of the House." The first two goddesses mentioned, Mnasa and the one referred to simply as the "Mistress," probably represent local divinities derived from the great goddess of the pre-Hellenic religion. Posidaeia is a feminine consort of Poseidon and may represent a coupling of the

100

great goddess with the patriarchal god, Poseidon, who when introduced by the Hellenes, became the spouse of an antecedent non-Greek goddess.

On the obverse we find two women named G $_{ʷ}$ owia and Komawenteia, who may have been participants in a ritual. Chadwick writes, "*Qo-wi-ja* [G $_{ʷ}$ owia] is apparently from *g $_{ʷ}$ ous* 'ox'; acrobats for the bull games?"[24] This ritual, if that is what it is, takes place at the shrine of Poseidon, one of whose sacred animals was a bull. Then parallel to the record on the reverse, we find the sacrifice of victims at a shrine of a triad of goddesses—Perse, Iphemedeia, and Diwia—and Hermes is joined with them, as the *Thrice-hero* was on the reverse. Chadwick suggests that Perse may be the goddess whom Homer mentions in the *Odyssey* as daughter of Oceanus and wife of Helios.[25] Helios, of course, is the sun-god and, therefore, Perse, his wife, might well have been a moon-goddess appropriately honored at the end of a solar-lunar cycle. We know from Homer that Iphemedeia was the mother of the twins, Otus and Ephialtes, by Poseidon. Here again is a variant on the archetype of the solar twins and Hermes, as transcendent third, makes sense in this context. Diwia is a feminine counterpart of Zeus as Posidaeia is of Poseidon. The untranslated word *Areia* following Hermes is probably another epithet, but its meaning is uncertain. It is tempting to see in this an epithet for Hermes meaning "the slayer of Argos," but that is conjecture.

There remains on the obverse the sacrifices performed at the shrine of Zeus. Here both Zeus and his classical consort, Hera, are honored. But a significant third figure also appears, Drimios, called "the son of Zeus," who is offered a gold bowl. Drimios is unknown in classical times. But in the context of a New Year festival as "son of Zeus," he might well represent the New Year babe, or succeeding sun-king. If so, Hermes is appropriately associated with him, since Hermes, as it will be shown, is the bringer of the New Year babe.

The Thrice-Hero was known at Pylos in the thirteenth century B.C., and he is symbolically represented as a "herm" between two pillars on more than a few Cretan icons of Late Minoan date. But is there any visual representation of him as a "hero" in the Bronze Age, before he was invested by the Greeks with the attributes of the classical Hermes? I believe it can be shown that there is such a figure.

The great goddess so dominates Minoan iconography that representations of a male figure in anything other than an attitude of adoration or subordination to the feminine deity are very rare. One exception is a recurring motif of a male figure who has been called the "Master of the Animals" for lack of a more adequate title. R. W. Hutchinson describes him as "a youthful figure usually depicted grasping two lions or other animals or birds by the throats."[26] Little or nothing is known about his significance other than the fact that he repeatedly appears in a central position between two beasts. But this in itself appears significant, in the light of the evidence we have seen of the Thrice-Hero as the central and dominant member of a trinity.

A Cretan seal of uncertain date, but probably Late Minoan, provides some interesting clues. (AM. 1938.1054) Here he is shown in a Minoan tight belt and short kilt in a central position between two identical lions, over whom he extends his arms as if in dominance (Figure 39). Since the lions are known to be solar calendar beasts in Crete and since they are here identical, they can be appropriately interpreted as the twin solar kings of the year. The central figure's dominance of them is precisely what we should expect of the Thrice-Hero, who is the transcendent form of both. His identification as the Thrice-Hero is further reinforced by the fact that he wears a crown of three sun disks and there are three diagonal parallel bars behind him in the field. His crown indicates that he is the sun-king as three-in-one and the three parallel bars recall the motifs in which he appears as a "herm" between twin pillars.

One significant detail remains to be noted. The twin lions are symmetrically similar but not precisely identical, since one has his left hind leg raised while the other raises his right hind leg. This is a variation on a motif discussed in the previous chapter. There we have seen examples of the Dioscuri, the solar twins of Sparta, represented as pillars of a shrine—each with the opposite heel raised to avoid contact with the earth. The significance, as we have seen, is that each reigns as a king in opposite halves of the solar year. Between the Dioscuri we frequently find a central member—usually some variant on a pillar. The archetypal

FIGURE 39. Late Minoan Cretan seal. The so-called "Master of the Animals." Note the crown of three sun-disks, the three parallel bars in the background, and the raised legs of the lions. (AM. 1938.1054.) *Ashmolean Museum.*

parallel with the figure of the Thrice-Hero on the Minoan gem is surprisingly close and complete. By what name the Thrice-Hero went among the Minoans before he became the Greek Hermes we do not know, but his calendric and religious significance is considerably clarified beyond what is implied by the enigmatic and misleading title "Master of the Animals."

At this point I should like to ask what will appear to be an irrelevant question, but which, in fact, is not. The question is: "Why does popular folklore credit the stork with bringing babies into the world?" The ready reply will be "To avoid giving a candid answer to a question little children are likely to ask." So far so good, but why should it be the stork rather than some other bird or beast? At this point the question becomes interesting, and I believe we may find a credible answer by examining a rare bird of mythopoeic thought.

A bird particularly sacred to Hermes was the crane, just as the long-legged ibis, another water fowl, was sacred to his Egyptian counterpart, Thoth.[27] But it does not appear that the association was borrowed from Egypt by equating Hermes and Thoth. I have found that the crane is a frequent motif in Minoan art, and it is found in a context which makes its significance reasonably certain.

Hesiod tells us that when the cranes can be seen migrating south (about October 31 by our calendar), farmers in Boeotia know that the fall rains are coming and it is time to plant the winter wheat.[28] Likewise when the cranes return in the spring (about February 5), the rains have ceased and spring farm chores may begin. This, by the way, is still a

103

sign which Cretan farmers watch for as the mark of the beginning and end of the winter season. And a modern observer writes, " . . . the most exciting bird migration is that of the cranes, who fly in large flocks over Crete in a north-westerly direction in the spring, returning south-eastwards in October."[29]

The Minoans of the Bronze Age were well aware of this seasonal sign, as several seal engravings show. One seal from Knossos (HM. 1597) combines the calendar labyrinth motif, with which we are familiar, with an icon of a serpent over which four cranes fly in V-formation (Figure 40). Since Minoan serpent season, as the Knossos calendar shows, began about 3 November and ended about 4 February, it coincided almost perfectly with the migration of the cranes in spring and fall. This seal plainly tells us by its combination of calendar symbols and a seasonal symbol that the cranes are associated with the winter season.

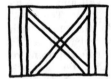  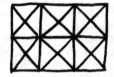

FIGURE 40. Sketch of seal design. From Knossos. Middle Minoan III (HM. 1597) This seal has a fourth face engraved with two standing birds. Illustration not available. Labyrinth motifs and serpent with cranes. *Heraklion Museum*.

Now, as we have seen, the winter season of the twin serpents is when, at winter solstice, Hermes, as one twin, dies, and as the other, is reborn. Consequently, in the going and coming of the cranes, the mythopoeic mind saw the going and coming of Hermes. It is probable that later classical tradition gave Hermes winged sandals, a winged hat, and, most significantly, a winged caduceus because he was associated not only with the two serpents, but also with the crane.

104

Another point of importance is that myth tells us that Theseus, after slaying the Minotaur in Crete, went to Delos where he danced the crane dance with youths and maidens around a horned altar.[30] This crane dance was surely a ritual and it probably occurred at the spring festival, when the cranes heralded the end of winter and the coming of spring. It is well known that Delos was the center of a solar-lunar cult and that the eight-year calendar cycle beginning with a winter solstice New Year was observed there.[31] In fact, according to classical tradition, it was in Delos that Leto gave birth to Apollo (the sun) and Artemis (the moon). Hence, it is certainly reasonable to infer that the crane dance was in celebration of a solar-lunar festival related to Hermes as crane.

Now we need only put together the pieces of the puzzle. Hermes manifests himself twice yearly as a crane. When he flies south at the end of October, the summer season of the lion ends and the sun, next represented by the serpent, declines until its death at the winter solstice. Then his twin, the serpent of the New Year, is conceived, but remains under the auspices of Hermes, the twin-serpent winter king, until early February when Hermes, the crane, appears again on the horizon flying northwest and bringing in the king of the waxing sun of spring. What is the function, then, of Hermes as crane? To escort the old king of the dying sun to the underworld and to bring in the New Year babe, the reborn king of the waxing sun. We know that in classical tradition Hermes was the conductor of souls to the underworld. It is only natural, therefore, to expect him to conduct newborn souls to this world.

That such was the function of Hermes is plain from a myth about the birth of Dionysus. Zeus, we are told, made love to Semele, the "moon," daughter of King Cadmus of Thebes. Hera in jealousy advised Semele, when she was six months with child, to demand that her lover show himself to her in his true nature and form. Semele, who had not recognized Hera as a goddess, and who did not suspect her plot, asked Zeus to appear to her in his true form. He refused, but she insisted and denied him further access to her bed. Then in anger Zeus appeared as thunder and lightning, and she was consumed. But Hermes, we are told, saved her six-months son. He sewed him up inside Zeus' thigh to mature for three more months, and in due time delivered him.[32]

Here Dionysus, who was called the "twice-born" or "the child of the double door" is the New Year babe. The myth has a Theban setting and appears to reflect a modification of the earlier moon-goddess worship by the religion of Olympian Zeus, since Zeus performs the function of a mother-goddess. As I read the myth, Dionysus was born first at the winter solstice, after a six-month course of the sun, and his second birth from the thigh of Zeus fell three months after at the spring equinox. The double door would be the two solar stations of the year. The New Year babe's spring advent would be a little later, then, than what appears to have been the custom in Minoan Crete. But the pattern is the same and it is Hermes who delivers the child.

It should now be obvious why the tenacious collective memory of folklore tells us that newborn babes are brought by the stork. The stork is Hermes who brings the reborn soul into the world. It is not a valid objection that a stork is not a crane. Neither is an ibis a crane, but that did not prevent the ibis of Thoth from being equated with the crane of Hermes. Both are large, long-legged, long-beaked water fowl, and so also is the stork. The mythmaker is no ornithologist. He thinks in terms of archetypes, not in terms of scientific distinctions.

The crane-Hermes of Crete was probably equated with the stork-Hermes of the Peloponnese by the pre-Hellenic Pelasgians. Classical myth tells us that Hermes was born in Arcadia. on the Peloponnese where the Pelasgians were the dominant people, and Strabo tells us that the Pelasgians who lived near Athens were known as *Pelargi,* meaning "storks."[33] It is likely that the stork was the totem bird of this particular Pelasgian tribe and was equated by them with Hermes. But whether as stork or crane or simply as Hermes his function was the same—to bring in the New Year babe.

There is, in fact, a Greek folk tale from the vicinity of Constantinople which suggests a link between Hermes as crane and Hermes as stork. Stated briefly, the story goes as follows. Three brothers—Dimitri, Michael, and George—set sail from a small village near Constantinople as members of

106

a ship's crew. They sail beyond the Straits of Gibraltar, whereupon a terrible storm drives them far from any known landfall. Finally, however, they reach an unknown land. Here the three brothers become separated from the rest of the crew, and, after crossing a great plain, they come in sight of a magnificent castle which appears to be empty. They enter it and find a feast spread in a banquet hall, and being unable to make anyone hear, they sit down and eat. But suddenly a great dragon appears who promptly catches Dimitri and Michael and devours them raw. George alone, being nimble, escapes and continues to outwit the dragon, who is blind, by passing out of the castle gate under the fleece of a ram in the manner of Odysseus' escape from the Cyclops. George then wanders through woods and across a plain until he comes to another castle surrounded by a town.

In due time he is brought before the king of the castle, who treats him kindly. In the presence of the king, he witnesses a very strange sight. The king orders various bands of his subjects to march forth to people the many distant countries of the world. They set off in groups and plunge into a broad river from which they emerge on the other side as so many bands of storks. George now awakes to the fact that this is the land of the storks! Six months later he witnessed their return. They dove into the same river and emerged on the near side as men. George asked the king to let him return to his native village, but the king replied that it would be impossible unless he would consent to become a stork. George agreed, dove into the river, and came out on the other side as a stork. He then flew back to his parents' home and, taking a stork as mate, built a nest on the roof of the house. He was so tame that he became the family pet, but he could not communicate, try as he would, the fact that he was really their long lost George. He decided, however, to play a trick upon his sister. She had a pair of silver armlets, one of which he managed to carry off and hide in his nest.

When fall arrived the storks migrated back to their own land and George went with them. He then begged the king to let him return permanently to his own village as a man. The king consented and sent him off in a specially built ship. The ship passed through a long dark channel and, at first, George could see nothing, but finally something like a dis-

107

tant star appeared, which proved to be daylight at the end of the channel. The ship emerged and George eventually reached his home. His parents were delighted to see him and asked about his adventures. He told them that among other wonderful adventures, he had once spent a season with them as a stork. Naturally they thought this a great joke, but George sent a servant to the stork's nest on the roof, telling them that he would find there the silver armlet he had hidden from his sister. And, just as he had said, the servant brought back the armlet to the amazement of all.[34]

The mythic content of this folk tale is not difficult to discern. The three brothers parallel the twin kings plus Hermes. They sail beyond the Pillars of Hercules where myth traditionally located the land of the dead. The twins—Dimitri and Michael—succumb to the dragon, who is death, but George, like a Hermes, survives death. George's escape from the blind dragon under the fleece of a ram is borrowed from the *Odyssey* or some cognate story that was probably old in Homer's time. It may have originally meant the survival of the sun-king's soul as sacred ram. At any rate, George, like Hermes, survives and reaches the kingdom of departed souls. And this kingdom is, to his great surprise, the land of the storks! The king of this land regularly sends forth souls to repeople the countries of the world. The souls dive into a river and emerge on the other side as storks, an obvious rebirth symbol. But note that the stork is the bringer of new life to the world. George, consistent with his role as Hermes, is himself reborn as a stork. As a stork, he flies to his paternal home and builds a nest on the roof. I have personally observed how the storks are venerated in Burgenland in Austria, where they nest on the rooftops. They are considered a good luck bird and no one would think of disturbing their nests.

George's hiding of his sister's armlet is no part of the myth, but a folktale twist that makes the story charming. But the seasonal migration of the storks is, of course, a fact, and it parallels the migration of the cranes and accounts for the mythic association of Hermes, as sun-king, with both. George's rebirth as a man is also meaningful. The long dark channel from which he emerges into daylight is a transparent symbol of rebirth from the womb. And, although he is not literally delivered to his parents by a stork, it is significant that as a stork he heralded his own rebirth.

Let us now look at an icon featuring a crane in a context with which we are familiar. A bronze relief from Perugia of the sixth century B.C. represents the Gorgon, Medusa (Figure 41). Medusa appears in the center of the relief flanked by two lions. The two lions represent the twin sun-kings and even have alternate hind legs raised in the manner of the Dioscuri. Above on the right is a sea horse with a fish-tail. He is a variant on Pegasus and represents the departure of the soul of the sun-king, which is emphasized by his flying position above Medusa. Medusa herself has her thighs spread in a position suggesting the act of childbirth. Consequently the entire icon represents a calendric event—the death of the old solar-king and the birth of the new king. And on the far right appears a bird which is unmistakably a crane. It is, of course, Hermes who brings in the New Year babe. This icon also confirms our interpretation of the role of Hermes in the myth of Perseus and Medusa.

In Christian tradition, the archetype of the birth of the sacred king at the New Year is to be seen in the birth of the Christ child on a date, December 25, which is the fifth day after the winter solstice. This date was not fixed as the official birthday of Christ until the fourth century A.D. It was chosen because it was the birthday of Mithra, a sun-god of Persian derivation who had a large following among Roman soldiers. Saint Chrysostom, writing in the early fifth century, and referring to the festival of the pagan Sun-god, says:

> On this day also the birthday of Christ was lately fixed at Rome in order that, while the heathens were busy with their profane ceremonies, the Christians might perform their sacred rites undisturbed. They call this [25 December] the birthday of the Invincible One [Mithra]; but who is so invicible as the Lord. They call it the Birthday of the Solar Disc; but Christ is the Sun of Righteousness.[35]

The question which arises is whether there is any remnant of the mythic role of Thrice Great Hermes in Christian iconography? I believe there is. The legend of the three

FIGURE 41. Bronze relief from Perugia. Sixth century B.C. Medusa between two lions. On the right,

kings following a star and bearing gifts to the Christ child at his solstice nativity is a Christian adaptation of the Thrice-Hero or Triple King, Hermes, attendant at the birth of the New Year babe. This identification is supported by a very early Christian icon. A stone ring, found at Naples, dating from the sixth century A.D. provides us with a pre-Medieval version of the three kings (Figure 42, p. 112). The Virgin sits with the Christ child on her lap, while behind her a shepherd points at the star. The three kings approach from the right bearing gifts. They are not dressed in exotic oriental garb, as they always are in Medieval versions. They are dressed alike in short, simple, classical tunics. It is difficult to tell from this crude engraving whether the appendages at their shoulders were meant to be wings or simply capes blowing in the wind. If they are wings, they would be appropriate to a Hermes represented in triad. The central king of the triad wears a pointed cap or helmet, which distinguishes him from the other two. Does his central position and his *petasos* identify him as the transcendent member of the triad? And is the star above, the planet Mercury (Hermes), which according to astrological lore is the ruling planet of the Zodiacal sign of Gemini, the twins? If so, Thrice Great Hermes survives to this day as the three kings from the East where the sun rises from the horizon.

Figure 42. Impression from a stone ring found at Naples. Sixth century A.D. The three kings bringing gifts to the Christ child who is the New Year babe.

CHAPTER VI

The Werewolf of Arcady and Captain Thirteen

After a severe drought had so dessicated the grasses of the hills and valleys of Arcadia that the shepherd's flocks were dwindling from starvation, Lycaon, king of Arcadia, sacrificed a child to Zeus Lycaeus in hope that this offering would bring them rain. Far from being pleased by the human sacrifice, Zeus in anger at such a barbarous act, struck Lycaon with lightning and turned him into a wolf for nine years.

But despite this obvious sign of divine displeasure, the sons of Lycaon, whom some say were twenty-two in number and some say fifty, continued their barbarous rites. When news of these practices reached Zeus on Olympus, he disguised himself as a traveling beggar and visited the sons of Lycaon in person. They served him a meal which contained the innards of sheep and goats, and also the entrails of their brother, Nyctimus, whom they had sacrificed. But Zeus was not deceived and, thrusting away the table upon which the meal had been set, turned them all into wolves, except Nyctimus, whom he restored to life.

When Zeus returned to Olympus, he was so angry with the entire race of man, whom by the way were all descendants of Pelasgus, father of Lycaon, that he sent forth a great flood to wipe out all of humanity. But one man and woman, Deucalion and his wife, Pyrrha, had been warned in

113

advance by Prometheus, the Titan, and, having built an ark, they survived the flood, coming to rest finally on the slope of Mount Parnassus. Thereupon they peopled the world anew.

However, the flood failed of its purpose, since some of the Parnassians wandered to Arcadia, where they revived their ancient rites.[1] According to Theophrastos (c. 322 B.C.), the Arcadians of his own time still sacrificed a boy to Zeus Lycaeus on Mount Lycaeum, his sacred mountain, in celebration of the festival of the New Year. The boy's entrails were mixed with the guts of sacrificed animals and served to the members of the clan of Anthos, who assembled at a sacred oak tree beside a stream. The person among the group who happened to eat the human sacrifice hung his clothes on the sacred oak, dove into the stream naked, and emerged on the opposite bank transformed into a wolf. Thereupon he joined a pack and ran with the wolves. If as wolf, he refrained from eating human flesh for nine years, the legend has it that he could return to the stream at the expiration of the period, dive into it, and emerge on the other side as a man once more and could don his clothes which he left hanging on the sacred tree. It is even reported that a certain Damarchos, an Arcadian, lived nine years as a wolf, regained his humanity, and thereafter won the boxing prize at the Olympic Games.[2]

This myth and its lingering legend in mountainous Arcadia is particularly interesting because Arcadia was the original homeland of Pelasgus and of the Pelasgian people, who were pre-Hellenic tribes that inhabited not only the Peloponnesus, but a large part of Greece proper as well as numerous islands of the Aegean before the coming of the Greeks. Strabo writes, "As for the Pelasgi, almost all agree, in the first place, that some ancient tribe of that name spread throughout the whole of Greece . . . . "[3] Strabo continues by citing a number of ancient authorities who attest that the Pelasgians were the earliest inhabitants of various places in Greece and the Aegean including Mycenae, Argos, Thessaly, Epirus, Athens, the Troad, and the islands of Lesbos, Lemnos, and Imbros.

These Pelasgians together with the Minoans of Crete provided the cultural base which underlies Mycenaean and Trojan civilization and ultimately classical Greek civilization, the latter being modified rather drastically by the Dorian invasions and a subsequent formative period known as "the dark ages." The exact relationship between the Minoans and the Pelasgians is unknown, but they certainly shared many contacts as close neighbors. The myth of Deucalion's flood implies a connection with Crete, since Deucalion was said to be the brother of Cretan Ariadne, daughter of King Minos.[4] By Homer's time, at least, if not far earlier, Pelasgians made up a part of Crete's rather mixed population.[5] We have already seen more than a little evidence that the Greeks of the earliest migrations, who settled amongst pre-Hellenic people, adopted a religion regulated by a ritual calendar, much like that of Minoan Crete. This is especially detectable in Arcadia.

Let us now look at the Arcadian wolf myth related of Lycaon, son of Pelasgus, whom Hesiod calls "god-like Lycaon."[6] Like so many myths we have examined, this one has two layers, a foundation layer derived from a Pelasgian ritual and a transparent upper layer, superimposed by a later Greek Olympian religion. The name Lycaon comes from the Greek word for "wolf" and so Lycaon is a wolf-king. Mount Lycaeum, where the child sacrifice was made, is therefore "Mount Wolf." And Zeus, except in this Arcadian cult, was never considered a Wolf-god. Now the sacrifice took place at a New Year festival and was intended to restore fertility to the grazing lands, so we are dealing with a god who is associated with the New Year and is also a fertility god. By a fortuitous coincidence, the name Lycaon approximates the sound of the Greek word for "light," which would be appropriate to a Wolf-god who was also a Sun-god. And since one of the sons of Lycaon was called Nyctimus, which means "night" or "of the night," it seems probable that Lycaon was a sacred solar-king. It then appears that Zeus Lycaeus is Olympian Zeus in name only, being, in fact, a solar wolf-king related to a ritual calendar.

We may understand, then, why Olympian Zeus was displeased with this sacrifice. His striking Lycaon with lightning and releasing a flood on his sons are signs not only of his anger, but of his proper function in Olympian religion as a rain-god and hurler of thunderbolts. But it was not Zeus who was really responsible for transforming Lycaon into a wolf or

115

turning his sons into a pack of wolves. Only the Great Goddess could perform these miracles at the solstices and she would have done so not in anger at the sacrifice, but in acceptance of it.

Indeed, in one version of the myth she does appear as Ge, the earth goddess, holding up both her hands to assuage the anger of Zeus at the child sacrifice. At least so the classical mythographer tells us.[7] But surely that is a mistaken notion of the mythographer, who has misinterpreted an icon of the Pelasgian fertility goddess, who like the Minoan goddess, is frequently shown holding up both hands in a gesture which displays her ten fingers, with a reference to the ten Dactyls or attendants on the sacred king (Figure 43). We are actually dealing with a variant on three known archetypes, the twin kings, the calendar totem beast, and the attendants upon the king.

The child is a surrogate for Lycaon and must die at the end of a solar-lunar cycle, so that the wolf-king may renew his reign for another great year. The fertility and well-being of the kingdom depend upon this renewal. Lycaon is reborn as a wolf. The wolf is the king's calendar totem beast, a variant on the bull or lion of Minoan Crete.

Mount Lycaeum would have been originally not Zeus' mountain, but the sacred mountain of the earth-mother as in Crete. And here she would manifest herself as a she-wolf, and moon-goddess, united in a sacred marriage with the wolf-king as solar king. The mythopoeic mind would have seen in the tendency of wolves to howl at the full moon, a confirmation of their wolf-king's love for the moon-goddess. In Minoan Crete she was never represented as a wolf, but she does appear as a collared bitch, who hunts the king as bull or stag at the solstice. Her canine image lies behind Cerberus, the three-headed hound of hell, and Hecate as we have seen. She does appear as a she-wolf in Rome where she nursed the twin kings, Romulus and Remus. As it has been pointed out, she holds up her ten fingers or "dactyls" in honor of the band of young initiates in puberty rites, who will be the attendants on the new born wolf-king. In this particular cult, they will have been initiated as wolves or, more exactly, as werewolves.

This is indicated in the myth when Zeus turns all of the

116

FIGURE 43. From Shrine of the Double Axes at Knossos (c. 1400–1100 B.C.) HM. Gallery X, Case 140. *Heraklion Museum*.

sons of Lycaon into wolves. The number of sons of Lycaon mentioned in the myth is the clue to their relation to the archetype of the attendants upon the king. Some said Lycaon had fifty sons and some said twenty-two. These are both calendar numbers. Fifty is the number of lunations in a four-year half-cycle of the eight-year solar-lunar calendar. Twenty-two is the number of moon phases in the spring or bull season of the Minoan calendar. Therefore, it appears that in Arcadia, the spring season of twenty-two moon phases was wolf season. The "sons" of Lycaon, aside from Nyc-

117

timus, who was actually sacrificed and reborn, would not be literally his sons, but the group of attendants upon the young prince, who were honorary wolves and sons. The nine years spent with a wolf pack would mean nine years of attendance on the wolf-king, until his reign should end at the summer solstice of the ninth year.

According to Pausanias, this legend and ritual was still alive in conservative Arcadia in his lifetime (second century A.D.).[8] The clan of Anthos who practiced this New Year ritual near Mount Lycaeum must have been descendants of Pelasgian stock who perpetuated the ancient customs of their forebears. At this late date, it is likely that they no longer sacrificed a child, but put a child selected by lot through a mock death ceremony and then partook of a ritual meal of sheep's innards, perhaps like the Scottish haggis. Then, one of the members of the group, again chosen by lot, probably went through a mimetic ritual removing his clothes and hanging them on the oak tree and then swimming across the stream, whereupon he would be initiated and known thereafter as a "wolf."

Regardless of how it may have been performed in detail, the symbolic intent of the ritual is clear. The oak is a sacred tree of life and of the renewal of life after death. In classical times it was the sacred tree of Zeus, who conveyed oracles through his sacred oak at Dodona. But in Pelasgian times, it would have been the tree of the great goddess nourishing man with its bountiful fruit. This is attested by Pausanias who says that Pelasgus, the first king, introduced as food the fruit of the oak, not of all oaks, but only the acorns of the eatable *phegos* oak.[9]

In the ritual the child of the old year suffers a mock death and then is eaten, or rather a sacrificed animal is eaten in place of him, so that his *mana* is transferred to his successor, the new year wolf-king. He, however, must die as a man and be reborn as a wolf. Accordingly he removes his human garments and dives into the stream, suffering a mimetic death by water and rebirth on the opposite side as a wolf. He has eaten the wolf-king's flesh as a man. Therefore, he may not eat men's flesh as a wolf. After a great year of observing this taboo, legend has it that he dives in the stream as wolf and is reborn once more as a man. Anyone

118

thus initiated was supposed to have taken in the *mana* of the wolf-king and therefore to possess a superior potency and strength. This magic probably gave rise to the belief that Damarchos won the Olympic boxing prize, because he had once been so initiated.

It also seems likely that the folktales about werewolves, well known in many places in Europe, originated in a misunderstanding of this ritual or a similar one, which would naturally enough be given a sinister twist by superstitious country folk. According to A. B. Cook, folktales about werewolves and about the ritual eating of human flesh, can be traced to this day in rural Arcadia.[10] The werewolf tales with which I am familiar feature the periodic transformation of a man into a wolf and of the wolf, once more, into a man. They therefore present a very close parallel with this ancient myth of the periodic death and rebirth of the wolf-king.

The persistence of the archetype of calendar totem beasts could be illustrated by many a folktale still current in the rural areas of Greece. Let us look at one from the Ionian island of Zacynthos—once a part of the kingdom of Odysseus. It is known as the story of Captain Thirteen.

In the time of the Hellenes there once lived a king, who was the strongest man of his day; and the three hairs on his breast were so long that you could take them and twist them twice round your hand. Another king once declared war against him, and on a certain month the fighting began. At first the other king was victorious; but afterwards the strong king with his army beat the enemy and pursued them to their town. He would there and then have destroyed them all, had they not given 400,000 dollars to his wife, who betrayed him and cut off his three hairs. This made him the weakest of all men. The enemy then took him prisoner, bound him, shut him up in a fortress, and gave him only an ounce of bread and an ounce of water a day. However, his hairs soon began to grow again. So Captain Thirteen—that was his name—and thirteen of his companions were flung by the enemy into a pit. As he was the last to be flung in, he fell on the top of his companions and escaped death. But his enemies then

119

covered the pit with a mountain. On the second day after he was thrown into the pit he found a dead bird somewhere. He stuck its wings on to his hands and flew up. He knocked his head on the mountain and sent it spinning up to the sun. He then flew further afield and soared high into the air. But a rain-storm came on and softened the clay, with which he had stuck the feathers on. So Captain Thirteen fell into the sea. Out came the sea-god and with his three-pronged fork gave him such a blow that the sea turned red with his blood, and changed him into a big fish, a dolphin. He told him too that he could never change back again till he found a girl willing to marry him. Now the sea in which the dolphin lived was of such a sort that no ship entering it could get out again. It so happened that a king and his daughter came that way. They got in easily enough but couldn't get out again; and so fearful a storm overtook them that their ship broke up. Nobody was saved but the princess and the king; for the dolphin took them both on his back to a small island, and then set them ashore on the coast they had come from. The princess resolved to wed the dolphin, and, to get him up to her castle, had a big canal dug from the sea to it. When all was ready for the wedding, the dolphin shook off his skin and changed into a young man of gigantic strength and great beauty. He married the princess, and they lived happily ever after.[11]

In this folk tale, as it is told today, there is no explanation of why the hero is called "Captain Thirteen." Yet he is very explicitly so called, and we may also note that he has exactly thirteen companions. And why is thirteen considered an unlucky number? If one were a Bronze Age fertility king, the answer would be, because on the third intercalated thirteenth month, one could expect to be ritually slain. Captain Thirteen is a king, and we are told that he is the strongest man of his day. A fertility king is accounted the strongest man of his people, because the *mana* of the tribal totem beast is vested in him. It would appear, then, that a myth about a fertility king lies behind the folktale.

There is, in fact, evidence of a somewhat parallel myth

120

reported by Pausanias. In his description of Athens, Pausanias writes,

> Behind the Lyceum is the tomb of Nisus, king of Megara, who was slain by Minos. The Athenians brought his body and buried it here. A story is told of this Nisus that he had purple hair on his head, and that he was doomed to die whenever it should be shorn. When the Cretans came into the land they carried the other cities in Megaris by storm, but laid siege to Nisaea in which Nisus had taken refuge. Thereupon, it is said, the daughter of Nisus fell in love with Minos and sheared her father's hair. So runs the tale.[12]

The king's strength being vested in his royal purple hair and his betrayal by a woman, in this case his daughter, to a rival king reflects a myth similar to the folk tale in these points. Therefore, it is not unreasonable to see in the folktale a mythic background.

We are told in the tale that "on a certain month," the king begins to fight with another king. At first the other king is victorious, but later Captain Thirteen makes a comeback. This can only mean that Captain Thirteen is king of the waxing year, and that the certain month when his fight began with the king of the waning year was the month of the summer solstice. At first the other king is victorious because the sun begins to wane at the summer solstice, but later he makes a comeback after the winter solstice.

However, at the following summer solstice, at the zenith of his ascendence over the other king, he is betrayed by his wife, the queen. She is given 400,000 dollars to betray him. The American currency is rather a surprise, but the amount is mythically right, being a sum divisible by four and, therefore, reflecting the four-year half-cycle of the ritual calendar. Her way of betraying him is also mythically right. Like Nisus and like another mythical hero, Samson, his strength is in his hair and she cuts the three long hairs from his chest, after which he becomes the weakest of men. In the original myth, his wife will have been the moon-goddess to whom he must be sacrificed. Since his name is Captain Thirteen, the three hairs must stand for the three intercalated thirteenth months in an eight-year cycle. Her "cutting" the hairs refers to the fact that the three intercalations permit her, as the moon, to catch up with him, as the sun-king, and, hence, it is said to weaken him.

Having been shorn and weakened, he is easily captured and imprisoned. The ounce of bread and ounce of water a day that he is given must refer to the fact that after the intercalations, the sun begins once more to gain little by little and day by day upon the moon. This is also the meaning of the statement that his three hairs began to grow again. He and his thirteen companions are then thrown into a pit and the pit is covered with a mountain. The thirteen companions would be the attendants on a sacred king, one for each of thirteen months.

The pit later covered by a mountain must refer to the Mycenaean tholos type of tomb in which sacred kings were buried. These tombs, shaped like a beehive, were built by a three-stage process. First a great mound of earth was heaped up in the shape of a beehive. Then cut blocks of stone were put in place, using the earth as a mold and temporary support. Once the domed stone structure was all in place, it would be self-supporting. Then the earth was dug out from under the structure and heaped on top, to form a great mound as a monument. Hence, the folktale is accurate in describing the king's tomb as a pit, later covered by a mountain.

Next we are told that the king escaped death. He dons bird's wings and flies to the top of the beehive tomb and strikes the mountain and sends it spinning up to the sun. We are already familiar with the winged escape of the soul of the sacred sun-king. The soul of the Cretan Talos flew off as a partridge and in the Perseus myth, the king's soul escapes as winged Pegasus. His striking the mountain and sending it spinning to the sun is appropriate for two reasons. First, because the beehive tombs, as the Treasury of Atreus shows, had a circular hole at the top of the dome, above which was only the piled earth of the mound (Figure 44). This is the hole through which the king's soul escapes. Secondly the mountain "spins" to the sun, because the tombs of sacred kings were associated with the symbol of the spiral which, in turn, was associated with the sun.

(a)   (b)

FIGURE 44 *(a).* The interior of the Treasury of Atreus at Mycenae showing the opening at the apex of the beehive dome. *(b)* Spiral motif on the facade of the Treasury of Atreus. (c. 1400–1300 B.C.)

The winged soul of the king flies aloft and becomes identified with the sun. But his wings fall off and he plunges into the sea, where the sea-god strikes him so that the sea becomes red with his blood. The mythic sense is that the sun appears to set in the western sea, and at sunset, the red rays on the horizon turn the entire sea red. The sea-god turns him into a dolphin and tells him that he can never be a man again, unless a girl will consent to wed him. The totem beast of the sun-king in this case is the dolphin.

Now the sea in which the dolphin lived, which one could enter but not get out of, is the realm of life after death. The only way to escape this realm is to be reborn. But one must have a means of rebirth, and, hence, the stipulation of the sea-god that the dolphin-king can only become a man again if he can find a woman who will wed him, for which we must read in

i.e. womb/ sea

the further implication—a woman willing to become a mother.

He finds such a one in the princess. The canal leading to her castle, where he is reborn as a man, is an obvious sexual symbol and proves that she is his mother as well as his bride. The great goddess of Bronze Age myths was always considered both mother and bride of the sacred king. His fertility aspect is emphasized again at the end, since we are told that he was "a young man of gigantic strength and great beauty."

The dolphin associated with the sun is vividly illustrated by a silver-gilt plaque from Elis of classical date (c. 300 B.C.) (Figure 45). In the center, above, is the radiant face of Helios, the sun, flanked on either side by pairs of horses, who traditionally draw his chariot across the sky. There are four horses to represent the four years of the solar-lunar half-cycle. By classical times, as we shall see later, the four-year half-cycle had been adopted as the governing cycle for the Olympic Games at the sanctuary near Elis. Below the face of Helios is a sun-disk used as a stud fastening his cloak. At the bottom we see two sporting dolphins facing each other. The doubling of the dolphins stems from the conception of the bipartite solar year.

A related plaque of bronze of the same date which was also found at Elis is in the shape of a crescent moon (Figure 46). In the center is a lotus, flanked on both sides by lilies, flowers associated with the moon-goddess. This is a fitting complement to the sun-plaque, illustrating the tradition of the sacred marriage of the moon-goddess and the sun-king at Elis.

The dolphin as a solar calendar beast makes its appearance, however, much earlier than the classical period. Let us look at a Bronze Age icon from Crete (Figure 47). It is a seal found in a tomb at Mochlos and it is dated Middle Minoan III. (HM. 747) Within the circular field is a dolphin at the upper right moving in a clockwise direction as part of the circular motif. Below, moving counter-clockwise, is another dolphin in an antithetical position. Completing the circle at the left is a curved bough with twenty-six leaves. In the center is a stylized octopus with simulated arms. The arms are engraved in conjunction with six full circles, a crescent,

FIGURE 45 (above). A silver-gilt plaque from Elis (c. 300 B.C.).
Helios, the sun, flanked by four horses and with two dolphins
below.
FIGURE 46 (below). A bronze plaque from Elis (c. 300 B.C.). A crescent moon with the lotus and lilies of the moon-goddess.

and the upper dolphin, which has a large circular eye. The eight arms of the octopus are, therefore, associated with eight images. Within the field at the left is a sun-disk with nineteen rays.

FIGURE 47. Cretan seal from Mochlos of the Middle Minoan III Period. An octopus, sun and moon symbols, two dolphins, and a fertility bough. (HM. 747) *Heraklion Museum.*

The entire design has in some sense a solar-lunar significance, as the image of the crescent moon and the rayed sun indicate. The octopus as an eight-armed creature with its arms disposed radially might well be associated with the sun and its eight-year cycle. The bough with leaves is certainly a fertility symbol and it is usually related to solar kings. The two dolphins swimming in opposite directions would then appear to represent the twin solar kings. The abstract images disposed about the arms of the octopus are problematical. Two of them, however, appear to have a specific significance. The crescent is the crescent of the waning moon and the image adjacent to it on the left, with one circle eclipsing another, might appropriately symbolize the old moon crescent giving birth to the new. Are these not the two sisters who give birth to one another in the riddle of the Sphinx?

Two other features of the design may have calendric meaning. The sun disk has nineteen rays and the longer nineteen-year solar-lunar cycle may have been known to the Minoans as well as the eight-year cycle. The fertility bough has twenty-six leaves, if one counts what appears to be a small leaf on the inner side. The other leaves are all on the outer side. Perhaps this mark is merely the result of a slip of the engraving tool. If, on the other hand, it is intentional, the total of twenty-six leaves, which is twice thirteen, may be a double reference to the fateful thirteenth month, doubled because the dolphins are twin kings. Could it be that in this seal of c. 1600 B.C., we have come across a forerunner of our folktale hero, Captain Thirteen, the dolphin-king? The connection with Crete is not unlikely for the mythic tradition holds that the sun-god, Apollo, appeared as a dolphin to Cretan sailors and led them to Delphi, where he founded his famous oracle and made the Cretans his priests! Curiously enough Apollo Delphinios, Delphi, and dolphin are all derived from the Greek root "delphis" which means "the womb" and consequently the dolphin is the uterine beast, recalling again the story of Captain Thirteen.

CHAPTER VII

Atalanta's Race

King Iasus of Arcadia had long wished for a male heir, and
when his wife, Clymene, bore him a daughter, Atalanta, he
was so disappointed he left the child to perish in the wilds
near Calydon. But Artemis took pity on the abandoned child
and sent a she-bear to nurse her. She was later adopted by a
band of hunters and grew to womanhood, trained to a
strenuous life of hunting in the forest. In fact, she gained
fame throughout Greece by shooting the great Calydonian
boar at a hunt, in which she competed successfully with a
number of the strongest young men of Greece.

This fact so pleased her father, Iasus, that he recognized
her as his daughter and welcomed her home. To her displeasure, however, his first request was that she should take a
husband. Atalanta, who had an independent spirit and
boyish ways, had no wish to put herself at the disposal of a
dominating husband. She also remembered that the Delphic
Oracle had warned her not to marry. But since she did not
want to deny her father's first request, she consented to
marry on one condition. She agreed to marry any suitor who
could beat her in a footrace, but if the suitor should lose, she
was free to take his life. Many young princes of Greece competed with her and lost their lives, for she was light and
swift and tireless in a race and easily outran them all. Despite her Amazonian ways, she was a very attractive young
woman and a certain Melanion of Arcadia was so struck

128

with her beauty that he dared to risk a race with her. But first he invoked the aid of the goddess, Aphrodite. Aphrodite, of course, was ever displeased with anyone who affected to despise the rites of love. She therefore determined to punish the virgin Atalanta for her indifference to men. She gave Melanion three golden apples, telling him to let them fall one by one in the course of the race, knowing that Atalanta could not resist the temptation to stop and pick them up and would thus be more than a little delayed.

The race began and Melanion got off to a good start gaining a slight lead and Atalanta deliberately let him hold the lead for the time being for, like all champion distance runners, her way was to let her competitors spend themselves in the early stage of a race and then to finish strong, passing them when they were winded. But when she began to gain on him, Melanion dropped one of the golden apples and Atalanta, thinking she could easily catch him, stopped to retrieve it. In fact, it did not delay her seriously, for she was soon gaining on him again. Melanion dropped the second apple and Atalanta retrieved it too. But once more she made up for lost time and soon was pressing him hard again. He let the third apple fall and Atalanta, confident that she could catch up as before, stopped and picked it up. True, she gained on him with every stride, but now the finish-post had come in sight and every second counted. She put out a final burst of speed and very nearly caught him, but it came a bit too late and Melanion passed the post with her behind him by no more than the length of a finger. And so, reluctant though she was, Atalanta took Melanion as her husband and he through her became heir to the throne of Iasus.[1]

This myth contains elements of an archetype with which we are already familiar. A young woman reaches marriageable age, engages in a contest, a footrace, and as a consequence is married to the victor and passes from maidenhood to womanhood. The myth plainly reflects an origin in a tribal *rite de passage*. But since Atalanta is a princess and heir to a kingdom, her marriage also involves the transferral of sacred kingship to Melanion by matrilinear succession. We may also safely assume that the previous suitors who lost to her and lost their lives were surrogate victims for the sacred king, her father, who thereby prolonged his reign.

129

That Atalanta was suckled by a she-bear, a beast traditionally sacred to Artemis, and that she grew up as a virgin huntress is appropriate for her in her maiden stage of life. In this stage she was a devotee of Artemis, who was a moon-goddess and virgin huntress, wielding a crescent-moon-shaped bow. The classical Artemis was derived from one aspect only of the great fertility goddess of the Bronze Age. She represents only the initial phase, the new moon, of the five phases of the moon-goddess apparent in the Knossos calendar.

Melanion's name means "dark moon-man," which I suspect indicates that he was fated to play the part of the sacred sun-king, lover of the pale white moon-goddess.[2] Perhaps he is called "dark" moon-man because the eight-year cycle ends at the phase of the dark of the moon, the next cycle beginning with the new moon crescent which follows. He wins Atalanta's hand by a stratagem suggested by Aphrodite. This is most appropriate because Aphrodite was also originally but one aspect of the great goddess, her embodiment as nubile nymph or sexually mature woman. In coming under her spell, Atalanta is not really failing in allegiance to the great goddess, but merely undergoing a process of growth, dying as "maiden" and being reborn as a wife and queen.

The golden apples Aphrodite gives to Melanion are the apples of immortality, for death and rebirth is the gift of the goddess to her mate, the sacred king. As we have seen, these are symbolically the same golden apples that another sacred king, Hercules, fetched from the Garden of the Hesperides. And in a mythic sense, they parallel the apple Eve gave to Adam in Eden, which also brought about an end to innocence, although, of course, Hebraic-Christian theology has given the mythic act a sinful significance, which the Bronze Age would not have understood.

In the light of mythic archetypes, it appears that the race of Atalanta and Melanion is based on an initiation ritual preceding marriage and that Melanion plays the part of the sun-king, while Atalanta represents the goddess as moon-queen. The stratagem by which Melanion wins her then takes on additional significance. The contest is a ritual enactment of the race of the sun and the moon in the eight-year solar-lunar cycle. Atalanta is the swifter runner, because the moon completes a lunar year eleven days before the sun completes a solar year. But as the Minoan calendar shows, the three intercalations of a thirteenth month in a sense cancel this advantage, allowing sun and moon a fresh start nearly neck and neck, as it were, at the time of the intercalations. Finally, however, Melanion wins the race but only by a finger length. This is appropriate as calendric symbolism because the eight year cycle does not permit a perfect reconciliation of solar-lunar time, but only a closely approximate one, since ninety-nine average lunations will cause the new moon to fall a little after (approximately a day and a half after, in years of maximum discrepancy) the winter solstice at the end of the cycle. It is therefore literally true that the sun completes the eight-year cycle just barely ahead of the moon, and that is the mythic meaning of Melanion's winning the race by a finger length.

Atalanta's race is in essence a mythical variant on the riddle of the Sphinx which Oedipus solved. The same basic calendar secret is stated in different terms. The difference is simply in the choice of metaphor, for whether we see the sun as pausing for the moon to catch up, as Oedipus put it, or the moon delayed so that the sun maintains a lead, is purely relative and immaterial from a mythic point of view. But we may be sure that Oedipus was correct in solving the riddle in terms of the sun rather than the moon, because the riddle included an additional factor—the intercalation of a single day every four years, which is strictly a solar intercalation. It is interesting to note as well that a variant on the myth of Atalanta states that she was a Boeotian princess rather than an Arcadian one and the Thebes of Oedipus, of course, was in Boeotia.[3] The myth of Atalanta's race therefore further supports the conclusion that the Bronze Age calendar of Boeotia, as well as of Elis, was much like the Minoan calendar.

The original significance of the myth no doubt had been forgotten by the time that the classical mythographers recorded it, for it has been turned into a tale of a wayward girl, unwilling to submit to male dominance who is eventually forced to conform with the wishes of her father and subject herself to the authority of her husband. The patriarchal twist that has been given to the myth derives from the Olympian religion in which the father-god, Zeus, replaced the great goddess of the Bronze Age.

The race of Atalanta is a contest which engages only two participants. In this respect it resembles the boxing match of Polydeuces and Amycus except, of course, that it involves a feminine competitor. However, the initiation and marriage rites, in which such contests had their origin, frequently involved the participation of a group of attendants upon the principals, the attendants, both male and female, being a select group chosen to represent the marriageable men and women of the entire tribe. Hence, the ritual celebration at a yearly festival could have three levels of meaning—a solstice marriage of the sun and the moon, a sacred marriage of the sun-king and the moon-queen, and the sanctification of tribal marriage at large by vicarious participation in the rites celebrated by the regal attendants. All three of these ritual meanings were originally inherent in the celebration of the Olympic Games and their counterparts elsewhere.

According to myth, the Olympic Games were founded by Hercules and the Dactyls who came from Crete to Olympia and there ran a footrace, the winner of which was crowned with wild olive.[4] Only Hercules and the male Dactyls figure in this myth. But the Dactyls, named after the fingers of the great goddess, were ten in all, five of which were female and sprang from her left hand, while the other five were male and sprang from her right hand. The males were, like the Curetes, attendants upon the sacred king, while the females were priestesses of the goddess and attendants upon the queen.

We know on the authority of Pausanias that a footrace for virgin girls was periodically included in the Olympic celebrations in classical times, although it occurred at a separate festival from the all-male events. It was said to have been originated by Hippodamia, princess of Pisa, in honor of Hera and in gratitude for the victory of Pelops in a chariot race, in which the young hero won her for his bride.[5] We shall look more closely at the account of this chariot race later. At the moment it is sufficient to point out that both sexes participated in these ritual games, which indicates their relatedness to the archetype of the attendants upon the sun-king and the moon-queen in a calendar festival.

132

Although the first officially recorded Olympiad did n
occur until 776 B.C., there is good reason to believe that the
games at Olympia began long before that date, and that they
owed their existence to ritual contests following in the main
the pattern of the Bronze Age rituals discussed above. There
are many parallels in myth and legend dating from the
Bronze Age such as the footrace run by the suitors of the
fifty Danaids of Argos, the race of the suitors of the daughter
of King Antaeus of Libya, and the race arranged by Icarius,
father of Penelope, in which Odysseus won his bride. Despite
local variations, what is common to all these rituals in their
original form is the mythic theme of the sacred marriage of
the moon and the sun, and the periodic celebration of this
union at a calendar festival by bands of youths and maidens
led by principals who represent the sun-king and the moon-
queen. In short, they all relate to the archetype of the attendants upon the king and queen and the ritual calendar
which governed the king's reign.

To fully appreciate the original significance of the
Olympic Games, we must first understand the prehistoric
character of the Olympian sanctuary and its relation to the
great goddess of a matrilinear society. Both archaeological
excavation and mythology provide evidence that the tradi-
tions of Olympia were built up gradually by the accretion of
layer upon layer of religious cult practices on sacred
grounds, which experienced over a thousand years of active
evolution. Although cult was superimposed upon cult right
down to the deification of the Roman Emperors, a recognizable continuity exists in that the later manifestations were
grafted upon the roots of the older and the successive divinities absorbed or transformed the significance of their
predecessors, enriching rather than confiscating the essential
continuity.

The sanctuary at Olympia appears to have had its origin
in an oracle of the earth goddess Ge or Gaea, which was
situated by a cleft in the bedrock of the hill, which at a later
date came to be known as the Hill of Cronus. Ludwig Drees
writes,

> Since the cleft of Ge was situated on the spur of the
> "Olympian mountains" it is quite possible that the

goddess of this sacred place was called "Olympian Ge," or "Ge on Olympia," or simply by her epithet "Olympia." In that case, the famous sanctuary would have taken its name from the cult; thus the goddess would have been named after the mountain and the sanctuary after the goddess. The sacred character of Olympia, like that of Delphi, was grounded in the cleft. From this it would follow that the earth goddess Ge was the oldest goddess at the sanctuaries of both Delphi and Olympia.[6]

Ge is an early pre-Hellenic prototype of the all-encompassing great goddess, whose many aspects gradually became differentiated under the names of separate goddesses representing distinct manifestations of the eternal feminine. When the feminine principle also came to be associated with the moon, appropriate aspects of the great goddess were equated with particular phases of the moon.

We have already seen that classical Artemis was derived from the goddess as new moon and maiden, and that Aphrodite was derived from her second phase as waxing moon and nymph. Hera derives from her third phase as full moon and as wife and mother. As the Minoan calendar shows, she had five phases in all as a moon-goddess. Her fourth phase as waning moon and elderly midwife was represented at Olympia by the shrine of Eileithyia and the serpent sun-child, Sosipolis.[7] This shrine, built into the Hill of Cronus like a cave, was one of the earliest structures of the Altis at Olympia. It corresponds with the mountain caves of the great goddess in Minoan Crete and is emblematic of the womb. Eileithyia, a Cretan goddess of childbirth, was the prototype of the matronly classical Demeter of Eleusis. At Olympia an old woman, annually chosen, was priestess of her shrine and she brought lustral water to wash the infant god, who was yearly reborn. Locally, he was called Sosipolis, "Savior of the City," and his theriomorphic form was a serpent. As the New Year sun-king born at the winter solstice in what was Minoan serpent season, he was naturally a serpent. The dark of the moon, the fifth and last phase, gave rise to the classical Hecate, the goddess in her death aspect. Thus, as moon-goddess she had five phases in all.

But before her association with the moon, she was the

chthonic earth mother, Ge, who took life and gave rebirth, and who, as we have seen, was the earliest divinity at Olympia. Later Ge was also built a sanctuary, called the Metroon, the shrine of the earth mother.[8] It is therefore apparent that long before Zeus took over the principal position at Olympia, the sanctuary was dedicated to the rites of the great goddess and her child, who would have been a sacred sun-king.

The race of the virgins of Hera may be understood in this light. We are told by Pausanias that Hippodamia called together sixteen of the most respected matrons of Elis to organize and oversee this feminine ritual. Three age groups participated, but apparently all were of marriageable age, for Pausanias calls them "maidens" and specifies that "they all run with their hair down their back, a short tunic reaching just below their knees and their right shoulder bare to the breast."[9] The winners were awarded a crown of olive leaves and a part of a heifer sacrificed to Hera. The identification of the maidens with the mother goddess Hera, their celebration of the marriage of Pelops and Hippodamia, and their preparation and supervision by married women all point to a ritual of initiation to the status of womanhood and a symbolic role for the winners, or perhaps the eldest of the winners, as spouse of the sun-king for the ensuing four years. The winner would become chief priestess of Hera and the other participants her attendants.

The priestesses of Hera are virgins for two reasons. First, because as myth tells us, Hera, although she was both wife and mother, renewed her virginity yearly by a ritual bath. Secondly, because the race does not honor virginity in itself, but is rather a *rite de passage* symbolizing the end of maidenhood and an initiation to womanhood. The winners of the race are crowned with olive leaves because the olive is the tree of life, representing the goddess as bearer of fruit. They partake of the ritually sacrificed heifer because, as moon-cow, Hera was the mate of the solar-bull. They are initiated by sixteen matrons, according to Pausanias, because one matron was chosen from each of the sixteen cities of the Eleans.[10] The footrace of the virgins, then, corresponds with the rituals performed by the archetypal attendants upon the moon-queen.

135

But what about the young men's footrace which myth tells us was first run by the male Dactyls, supervised by Hercules who brought them from Crete? First of all we must recognize that we are dealing here with a Cretan Hercules and not with the later Greek hero, the son of Zeus by Alcmene. Cretan Hercules or Herakles derived his name from Hera, the moon-goddess, who was his mother. In Minoan Crete, he was the leader of a band of Dactyls, who were also known as Curetes as we have seen. Cretan Hercules was therefore not a particular mythical hero, but the symbolic title given to the principal in a ritual ceremony performed by selected young men who had reached marriageable age, and who celebrated the *rite de passage* initiating boys to the status and duties of manhood. This "Hercules" was chosen by a test. He was the winner of the men's footrace at Olympia, which occurred every four years. In short he was the male counterpart of the moon-queen chosen by the virgin footrace. He represented the sun-king, bridegroom of the moon-queen for the ensuing four years of the solar-lunar half-cycle. He was therefore crowned with olive leaves as spouse of the goddess. After his victory, he led a procession to the altar of the goddess where a bull was sacrificed. The sacrificed bull was a surrogate, the solar-bull, for the previous "Hercules" of the past four years and was killed like a sacred king at the end of his reign.

One further detail of the men's race deserves mention. According to Phlegon of Tralles, a contemporary of Pausanias, the victor in the men's race was originally not awarded a crown of olive leaves, but "the fruit of the apple."[11] This is interesting indeed if we recall the race of Atalanta. Aphrodite gave Melanion three golden apples which in turn Atalanta retrieved. The apple of immortality was originally the gift of the moon-goddess to her bridegroom, the sun-king. When the winner of the men's footrace at Olympia received the apple as prize, it was a token of his eventual rebirth but also of his demise within four years.

Each independent city-state of classical Greece had its own local calendar, but since the games at Olympia were panhellenic, it became the practice of historians to date events in Greek history at large in terms of Olympiads, the four-year periods of the Olympic Festival. According to a document preserved by Comarchos, the reckoning was made by a system which calls for some interpretation.[12] It was based upon a starting point at the winter solstice. The method was to take the first full moon after the solstice and count forward to the eighth full moon following for the date of the festival. Using the first official Olympiad as an example, this will give the full moon (August 22, 776 B.C.) of the Elean month of Apollonios as the central day of the first celebration. The next will fall four years later, after fifty months, at the full moon (September 6, 772 B.C.) of the month of Parthenios. The next celebration will come forty-nine months later at the full moon (August 23, 768 B.C.) of Apollonios once more, and so on.

This system proves beyond doubt that the festival was determined by an eight-year solar-lunar calendar which closely matches the Minoan calendar. It is a movable feast, because it must occur at full moon in honor of the moon-goddess. Since eight solar years amount to ninety-nine lunations, it becomes necessary to hold the festival alternately at intervals of fifty and forty-nine months. That the reckoning is made from a starting point at winter solstice indicates that this was originally the New Year at Elis, as it appears to have been also in early days in Boeotia, Delos, Delphi, and Athens. This coincides with the winter solstice New Year of the Minoan calendar. Furthermore, the timing of the most important festival of the solar-lunar great year parallels the practice in Minoan Crete. As we have seen, the Minoan king's reign came to an end, not at winter solstice of the eighth year, but at full moon of the seventh lunation following. The Olympic Festival falls at full moon of the eighth lunation following the solstice and at the end of every four-year half-cycle. The fact that it falls alternately in the Elean months Apollonios and Parthenios is also significant. Apollonios takes its name from Apollo, the sun, and Parthenios from the "maiden," namely the maiden-moon. Hence, the two principals of the sacred marriage are honored.

Now the women's games took place in classical times at a different festival, the Heraea. These games were also geared to the four-year half-cycle, but with an interesting difference. They were always celebrated in the same month, at new moon of Parthenios. Therefore, in alternate Olympiads, the men's games fell fourteen days before, and fourteen days after the women's games.[13] It is appropriate that the race of the virgins occurred in Parthenios, the month of the maiden, and at new moon in honor of the virgin moon. But it is also interesting to note that the fourteen days between the two festivals parallels the fourteen-day festival, which appears to have been celebrated at Minoan Knossos at the end of a king's eight-and-one-half-year reign and in conjunction with a full moon falling at this time. The coincidence suggests that in very early times, the two festivals at Olympia may have been one.

In classical times one of the more spectacular events of the Olympic Games was the chariot race. Tradition held that this race celebrated the mythic chariot race of Oenomaus and Pelops to which I have previously alluded. Oenomaus, king of Pisa near Olympia, refused to marry off his daughter, Hippodamia, unless her suitor could beat him in a chariot race, and suitors who lost could expect to forfeit their lives. Thirteen princes had accepted the challenge but all had lost, for Oenomaus stabled the swiftest horses in Greece. Nevertheless, Pelops decided to make the trial. Before entering the race, Pelops sacrificed to Cydonian Athena, and Hippodamia, who admired his looks and courage, decided to carry out a little plan of her own to help him. She secretly arranged to have her father's charioteer, Myrtilus, remove the linchpins from the axles of the royal chariot and replace them with wax ones.

The race course laid out by Oenomaus was a long one starting at Pisa and finishing at the Isthmus of Corinth. It was the king's practice to have Hippodamia ride in the chariot with the challenger, but he would give them a head start while he sacrificed a black ram to Zeus. It was also not an ordinary race to the finish, for if Oenomaus could catch the suitor's fleeing chariot, he could then consider the race won and dispatch the suitor by hurling a bronze spear into his back. This, indeed, is how he had killed all thirteen previous challengers. And so he might have done again, but just as he was catching up with Pelops, the wax linchpins gave way, the wheels of his chariot flew off, and he fell entangled in the wreckage and was dragged to death.[14] And so it was that Pelops won Hippodamia as his bride and the kingdom of

138

Oenomaus as well. Thereafter Pelops and his Mycenaean descendants so dominated the area that it came to be known as the Peloponnese or "the island of Pelops."

In the light of our previous examples, this myth of pre-Dorian date is quite transparent and its ritual content is plain. Once again we have a contest, this time a chariot race, upon the winning of which depends the prize of a bride and a kingdom, while the loser suffers death. It is a chariot race because the local totem beast of the sacred king is this time a horse, and also because the sun-god, Helios, was mythically conceived as racing across the sky from sunrise to sunset in a four-horsed chariot. His chariot, as we have seen, has four horses to recall the four years of the solar-lunar half-cycle. Oenomaus' daughter, Hippodamia, is so called because she is the "horse tamer." Hippodamia is, in fact, both a moon-queen and a mare. This association is attested by the later classical moon-goddess, Selene, who appears in works of art riding upon a white mare. Hippodamia is the moon-mare whom the sun-stallion races in the cycle of the calendar, and she has a head start because the moon completes a lunar year before the sun can complete a solar year. The thirteen unlucky suitors, who lost to Oenomaus, were sacrificed as surrogates in his stead, thirteen standing for the thirteenth intercalated month at the end of a cycle. Pelops, of course, is the succeeding sun-king who inherits the throne by matrilinear succession. He is able to win because he has the help of the goddess, Cydonian Athena, and her representative, the princess Hippodamia. Athena of Cydonia, a city in western Crete, was an Athena of the pre-Hellenic religion, a maiden fertility goddess.

Now let us look at two icons to test the validity of this interpretation. The first is a red-figured *amphora* now in the Museo Pubblico at Arezzo (Figure 48). It shows Pelops and Hippodamia fleeing together in a chariot drawn by four horses. Behind them in the background is an olive tree with eight branches. Before them in the background of the horses is another olive tree with only four branches, and two doves are perched upon it.

The four horses are the four horses of Helios, the Sun. The olive trees appear because they are sacred to Athena, the fertility goddess to whom Pelops offered a sacrifice before

FIGURE 48. Red-figured *amphora* from Museo Pubblico in Arezzo. Pelops and Hippodamia. (c. 425-400 B.C.)

the race. Pelasgian Athena, by the way, was reported to have brought olive culture to the Athenians and she planted a sacred olive tree on the Acropolis by the Erechtheon. To return to the illustration, one tree has eight branches to signify the eight-year cycle while the other has four to signify the four-year half-cycle. The two doves are sacred to Aphrodite and they appear here to suggest the union in love of Pelops and Hippodamia. The icon certainly supports the calendric interpretation of the myth.

A more complex icon illustrating the same myth appears on a *krater* from Apulia. The *krater* features two scenes from the myth, one on each side. One side shows Pelops and Oenomaus offering libations before a sacred pillar (Figure 49). The original significance of the sacred pillar, as we have seen, was as an emblem of the tree of life of the great goddess. Each is offering a libation to the divinity before the race in hope of victory. To the left is Hippodamia in bridal attire, wielding a curious scepter-like staff. The staff has crossed diagonals at the point where a double axe would be normally hafted on its shaft and the four ends and the staff itself are tipped with radiations. Since there are five radiant centers in all, I take this to be Hippodamia's scepter as moon-queen, one sparkling center for each of the five phases of the moon. The crossed diagonals suggest the double axe of the great goddess and also constitute a labyrinth motif. She is apparently mistress of the labyrinth of the calendar cycle and of the kingship for which the race will be run. Above her is the Greek letter gamma. This is puzzling but it is possibly meant to signify the sacred marriage or *hieros gamos* of the sun-king and moon-queen, the gamma being the initial letter in the Greek word for marriage, *gamos*. Beyond on the left sits Hercules. No doubt he is present as the mythic founder of the Olympic Games, to which this famous chariot race added an important event. At each end, to the left and the right, are tree trunks, recalling the sacred altis or grove of the fertility goddess, and doves, showing Aphrodite's presence as goddess of love. Finally, on the right there is Myrtilus, the charioteer, who removed the linchpins from the king's chariot.[15]

In the background are three circular figures, with smaller

FIGURE 49. A *krater* from Apulia. In the center, Pelops and Oenomaus offer libations before a sacred pillar. On the left are Hippodamia and Hercules. On the right is Myrtilus, the charioteer. *British Museum.*

FIGURE 50. Reverse side of *krater* from Apulia. Pelops slaying Oenomaus before an altar. On the right is Cydonian Athena. In the background, moon symbols indicate that the sacrifice takes place on the summer solstice. On the base of the altar are fifty-eight full-moon symbols to indicate the date of the Olympic Festival in classical times. *British Museum*.

circles arranged in a ring within the circumferences. The two at the right have thirteen small circles within, while the one at the left has eleven. The significant numbers are, then, three, thirteen, and eleven. The formula appears to be three intercalations of a thirteenth month in an eight-year cycle to equalize the eleven-day difference between solar and lunar years.

There are also three other figures in the background. Each appears to represent two full moons with crescent moons beneath. The total is six full moons and eleven crescents. Since the crescents face upward rather than left or right, they could stand equally well for new moon or old moon crescents. Now in six months, one will see six full moons and twelve crescent moons, the crescents being seen at both the beginning and end of each lunation. But here we have only eleven crescents. This must mean that the scene depicted on the *krater* takes place at the sixth full moon after a starting point at new moon, in which case only eleven crescents would have been seen. Now the Minoan calendar

144

shows us that an eight-year cycle ends at new moon on the winter solstice and the circular symbols tell us that we are dealing with just such a cycle. And since we know that the Olympic Games, with which this myth is connected, were celebrated at a full moon, reckoned from the solstice and following the end of a cycle, it follows that this combination of symbols is here to tell us when this particular scene took place. It took place at full moon five and one-half months after the solstice ending a cycle. This means that it would fall at the end of our first week of June or two weeks before the summer solstice. At first sight, this appears to be a surprising time for the event pictured to occur, but let us look further before judging.

The reverse side of the *krater* features a second icon which is instructive (Figure 50). Oenomaus, dressed in the ceremonial robes of a sacred king including the crossed rectangle or labyrinth motif on his chest, is being slain at an altar with a sword by Pelops. At the right of the altar, as if accepting the sacrifice, is a young goddess carrying two spears and a shield which appears to have a Gorgon's head upon it. Her raised right arm bears seven moon symbols and her legs are cross-gartered. Who is she? The answer is Cydonian Athena. Of this we may be sure for a number of reasons. Classical Athena carries a spear and a shield with the Gorgonian, but she does not go cross-gartered. But Cydonian Athena, like Artemis, was a huntress and such leggings would be appropriate for her. According to the mystic doctrine of the Pythagoreans, the symbolic number seven was known as "Athena."[16] This doctrine was derived from the Orphic mysteries and ultimately from Crete, where Pythagoras was said to have been initiated in the Orphic cult. We have seen that seven was a number especially sacred to the Minoan moon-goddess. The seven full-moon symbols on the goddess's raised right arm identify her as Cydonian Athena of Crete, who was a moon-goddess and whose sacred number was seven. Finally, the myth offers a further proof since we are told that Pelops sacrificed to Athena of Cydonia.[17]

Behind Athena is a small ram's skull with horns. But this is intelligible since the myth tells us that Oenomaus sacrificed a ram before the chariot race. In other respects,

145

however, the icon differs from the standard myth, for here we see Pelops slaying Oenomaus in a ceremonial way at an altar. In this version he is not killed in a chariot wreck. But I believe we may understand why if we go a bit further in interpretation.

Athena's right arm is raised in a significant gesture. She is pointing to a lunar symbol of the same kind that we saw on the other side of the *krater*. There are three of these symbols composed of full and crescent moons. But the count is different from what we found on the opposite side. There are six full moons and twelve crescents. This must mean that the event pictured takes place at new moon, a full six months after the winter solstice. Therefore it takes place two weeks after the scene on the other side of the *krater* and falls exactly on the summer solstice. Now we may understand the puzzling date given on the other side. The other side shows a ceremonial libation at the altar by the two contestants in hope of divine favor. It occurs fourteen days earlier because the midsummer festival, as the Minoan calendar indicates, lasted exactly fourteen days. The first scene, then, pictures the ritual at the opening of the festival while the second portrays the ritual at the end. Athena is pointing at a calendar symbol which has solar significance. Astronomically speaking, the king of the waxing sun should die at the hands of his tanist, the waning sun, not at the time of the classical Olympic Festival, but precisely on the summer solstice. And that is why we see here a ceremonial slaying of the king rather than a chariot wreck.

But what about the classical Olympic Festival itself, which was ultimately derived from the solar ritual? Is there any indication of the date of this later festival in the icon? The answer is yes. The base of the altar at which Oenomaus is being sacrificed is decorated with fifty-eight full moon symbols. Now we may recall that the classical Olympic Festival took place every four years or fifty lunations, plus an additional eight full moons. Plainly the fifty-eight full moons on the altar indicate the traditional date of the Olympic Festival in classical times.

It would be difficult to find a more convincing demonstration than this of the major thesis of this book, namely that the Knossos calendar and the archetypes it provides give us

146

a skeleton key that will open many doors to the meaning of myths and icons hitherto misunderstood or, at best, only partly understood. Many another myth and a multitude of extant ancient icons contain similar calendric symbolism, the significance of which remains quite unsuspected. The archetype of the attendants upon the king and related calendar implications lie not only behind the Olympic Games, but the other pan-Hellenic games as well—the Pythian, Isthmian, and Nemean Games. Indeed, as I write these lines, the modern version of the race of Atalanta is being run by young women at Munich in the 1972 Olympics. The Olympic torch has not yet been extinguished, but it is unlikely that many are aware that the maidens run in honor of the moon and the Olympic torch burns eternally in honor of the sun.[18]

CHAPTER VIII

The Lamb in the Labyrinth

A living folktale from Greece is recorded as follows:

There was once a king, who had three sons and great
riches; and, before he died, he divided his substance
among his sons. The two elder sons lived a merry life,
year in year out, squandering and scattering their
father's treasures till there was nothing left and they
were reduced to poverty. The youngest on the other
hand kept house with his share, took a wife, and had by
her a most beautiful daughter. When she grew up, he
built for her a big underground palace, and killed the
architect who had built it. Then he shut up his daughter in it, and sent heralds throughout the world to an-
nounce that, whosoever could succeed in finding the
king's daughter, should have her to wife; but that, if he
failed to find her, he must be put to death. So many
young men came to essay the adventure. But all their
efforts were in vain: they could not find the princess,
and they lost their heads.

After many had already met their deaths, there
came one young man, as clever as he was handsome,
bent on pursuing the quest. He went therefore to a
herdsman and begged him to hide him in a sheep-skin
with a golden fleece and to bring him in this disguise
before the king. The shepherd agreed to do so, took a

sheep-skin which had a golden fleece, sewed up the fellow inside it, gave him also food and drink and sheep's droppings, and so brought him before the king. The king, on seeing the golden lamb asked the herdsman: "Have you got that lamb for sale?" But the herdsman rejoined: "No, sire, not for sale; but, if it takes your fancy, I will gladly do you a service and lend it you without pay for three days. But you must then give it back to me."

The king promised to do so, and repaired with the lamb to his daughter. Having led it into his castle and through many chambers, he came to a door and cried: "Open, Tartara Martara of the earth!" Thereupon the door flew open of itself; and, after they had gone through many more chambers, they came to a second door. Here the king again cried: "Open, Tartara Martara of the earth!" Then the door flew open of itself; and they came to the room, where the princess lived. Its floor, walls, and ceiling were of solid silver. The king, when he had greeted the princess, gave her the lamb. She was delighted with it: she stroked it and fondled it and played with it. But when, shortly afterwards, the lamb eased itself, the princess said to the king: "Father, the lamb has eased itself!" And he replied: "It is just a lamb, why should it not?" Then he left the lamb with the princess and went his way.

During the night the young fellow drew off the skin. And the princess, seeing that he was so handsome, fell in love with him and asked: "Why did you hide in the skin and come here?" He replied: "When I saw that so many failed to find you and lost their lives, I contrived this trick and came to you." Then the princess exclaimed: "Oh, you have done well! But you must know that, even if you have found me here, your wager is not yet won. For then my father changes me and my maidens into ducks and asks you: 'Which of these ducks is the princess?' But I will turn my head round and plume my feathers with my beak, so that you can recognize me."

When they had prattled away for three days together, the herdsman came back to the king and demanded his lamb. And the king went to his daughter to fetch it. She was woe-begone at her sporting with the lamb being so soon over. But the king said: "I cannot leave it with you, for it is only lent." He took it away and returned it to the herdsman.

The young fellow now pulled off the skin, went to the king and said: "Sire, I can find your daughter." The king, seeing the handsome boy, answered him: "I'm sorry for your youth, my boy. This adventure has already cost so many their lives, and it will be the death of you too." "I stand by my word, sir king; I will either find her or lose my head." So saying, he went in front of the king and the king followed him till they came to the great door. Then said the young man to the king: "Speak three words, and it opens." And the king made answer: "What words are they? Shall I say: Lock, Lock, Lock?" "No," cried he, "say: Open Tartara Martara of the earth!" The king did so, and the door opened. They went in, and the king bit his moustache for anger. Then they came to the second door, where the same thing happened over again. They entered, and found the princess.

Next the king said: "Well done, you have found the princess. But now I am going to turn her and her maidens into ducks; and, if you can guess which of them all is my daughter, then you shall have her to wife." And without more ado the king changed all the maidens into ducks, brought them before the young man, and said to him: "Now show me, which is my daughter." Then the princess, as she had agreed to do, plumed her wings with her beak; and the young man answered: "The one yonder, pluming her wings, is the princess." There was then no help for it; the king had to give her to him for a wife, and he lived with her in grandeur and in happiness.[1]

This folk tale from Epirus is an interesting variant on the labyrinth archetype. The three brothers remind one of the three sons of Europa—Minos, Rhadamanthys, and Sarpedon—who quarreled and left Minos in sole possession of Crete. In the myth, Minos married Pasiphaë, who consorted with a white bull, the gift of a god, and bore the Minotaur.

Minos had Daidalos, the architect, build the mazelike labyrinth in which to conceal the Minotaur and Pasiphaë. When Minos discovered that Daidalos had constructed a wooden cow in which Pasiphaë had climbed in order to couple with the bull, he sought the life of his architect, but Daidalos escaped. The secret way into and out of the complicated labyrinth was known to few, among whom one was Minos' beautiful daughter by Pasiphaë, the princess, Ariadne.[2]

There are some obvious parallels in the folktale. One of three brothers, who inherit a kingdom, prospers while the others lose their share. The prudent brother marries and has by his wife, a beautiful daughter. He has an architect build him a palace with secret passageways and then has the architect killed to keep the secret. He hides, not a Minotaur nor a disgraced wife in the palace, but his marriageable daughter.

The parallels are plain, but the variations we find in the folktale may tell us some interesting things about the labyrinth which the mythic tradition lacks. In the folktale, we find that the palace is underground. We also find that its secret doors will open of themselves if one speaks the right words. The secret formula is: "Open, Tartara Martara of the earth." Our earlier discussion of the archetype revealed that the labyrinth is at once, and without contradiction, the underworld and the womb of the great goddess. The Greek word *Tartara* is the name for the deepest part of the underworld, if we give *Tartarus* a feminine ending as it has to this day in Rhodes.[3] There is no Greek word spelled precisely as *Martara,* but *mitera,* meaning "mother" is very close in sound and the context makes it clear that this is what is meant. The distortion is deliberate to make the word "mother" rhyme with *Tartara.* The rest is self-evident. The formula is not meaningless mumbo-jumbo. It means: "Open, Tartarus, womb of the Earth-Mother." Plainly, the labyrinth of this tale is in one sense the womb of Mother Earth. We have seen that the Cretan labyrinth had this significance as well, although one would not have suspected it on the basis of classical myth, in its literary form alone.

Although we are not told so, the king was no doubt reluctant to let his daughter marry because, if this story stems from an early myth, he would have been a sacred king who would have lost his throne to his daughter's husband. The folktale, as it stands, provides no motive for the king's behavior. If we assume that a myth of the kind we are familiar with underlies the folktale, a motive emerges, for the suitors who lost their heads would have been ritually slain in place of the king.

In this story we have a lamb in the labyrinth instead of a Minotaur. But note that it is a man in the skin of a lamb, so it is, in effect, a man-lamb just as the Minotaur is a man-bull. Myth tells us that when Atreus and Thyestes contended for the throne of Mycenae, the possessor of the golden fleece of a lamb that had been sacrificed to Artemis, was accounted the rightful king.[4] The totem beast of the solar king of Mycenae at this time was apparently a golden ram, and the golden fleece in the folktale must have originally had a similar significance. Appropriately, the young man, who is to become a solar king, finds his way to the princess in the fleece of a golden lamb.

The labyrinthine underground palace has many chambers and two magic doors. In the innermost room, he finds the princess who falls in love with him. She warns him, however, that he will not fully pass the test unless he can identify her, after her father has turned her and her maidens into ducks. The meaning of this is that the mistress of the labyrinth—the Ariadne, if you will—is in this instance a goddess whose epiphany was a duck. Just as in the myth, Ariadne helps her lover, Theseus, to survive the test of the labyrinth of Knossos, this princess helps her lover pass the test by pluming her wings so that he may identify her after she has been changed into a duck. Like Theseus, he passes the test and wins the princess.

We may now recall that on the Tragliatella wine jar, previously discussed, a horseman with a duck on his shield is shown emerging from a labyrinth shaped like a womb (Figure 13). The goddess as duck, or a similar water fowl, a goose or a swan, is mistress of the labyrinth. There the hero is united with her in a sacred marriage, but it is equally true that the goddess is his mother and the labyrinth is her womb. Their marriage union is as sun-king and moon-goddess in the solar-lunar cycle. In this story, the golden fleece

152

identify the hero as a sun-king while the silver room in which the princess resides identifies her as moon-goddess, for silver is the metal traditionally associated with the moon.

An icon of the classical period will confirm some of the conclusions reached thus far (Figure 51). It is a *kylix* showing Pasiphaë with the Minotaur as a child on her lap. Pasiphaë, whose name means "she who shines on all" was a moon-goddess and mother of the Minotaur of labyrinth fame. Myth does not tell us that the Minotaur was born in the labyrinth, but this icon does. The Minotaur is usually depicted full-grown, but here he is an infant on his mother's lap. We have no impression here of the terrible monster of popular fame. On the contrary, Pasiphaë lovingly holds her divine child in a pose which strikingly recalls later paintings of the Madonna and the Christ child. That the child was born, in a symbolic sense, from the labyrinth as womb is indicated by the hanging basket decorated with a checker-pattern, which, as previously mentioned, is a variant motif for the maze of the labyrinth.

Another such checker-pattern may be seen on the right margin, while above and below on the margin is the labyrinth motif of the crossed rectangle, which specifically suggests the solar-lunar calendar. On the right, where the border is fully preserved, we may count ten consecutive spirals above, interrupted by the checker-pattern, and then nine consecutive spirals below, terminated by the lower crossed rectangle. The count is nineteen spirals for the longer nineteen-year solar-lunar cycle. The left border is damaged and incomplete, but the spacing indicates that there were probably nineteen spirals there also. Another calendar number appears on the dias beneath the throne of the goddess. It displays eight and one-half patterned panels to represent the eight-year cycle, plus seven lunations at the end of which the sacred king must die. And at the foot of the goddess at the right, we find the bird of her epiphany, a goose. We know the basket, of course, as a variant womb symbol, and we have just examined a labyrinth tale in which the goddess is turned into a duck, here paralleled by a goose.

Another icon of the classical period offers additional insight (Figure 52). It is a painted vase from Nola, picturing an incident from a myth about Zeus and the Muse, Thalia.

FIGURE 51. A red-figured *kylix*. Pasiphaë with the Minotaur as a child on her lap. To the right, a basket and a goose, *Bibliothèque Nationale, Paris*.

This myth of Sicilian origin tells how Zeus in the form of a vulture wooed the mountain-nymph, Thalia, on Mount Aetna. The mythographers appear to have equated this Sicilian nymph with the Muse of the same name. According to the myth, Zeus fathered on Thalia a pair of twins called the

Palikoi. She gave birth to these twins in the domain of the earth-goddess to whom Zeus had entrusted her.[5]

ΘΑΛΙΑ

FIGURE 52. A red-figured vase from Nola. Zeus as a vulture abducting the mountain-nymph Thalia. At the right, a basket with a checker-pattern and four spirals and above it, a ball of thread. Formerly in the Hamilton collection.

As usual the icon and myth considered together will help to solve some problems hitherto shrouded in mystery.

The vase shows Thalia, who is identified by name, being carried off by Zeus as a bald-headed vulture. The bird of Olympian Zeus is usually an eagle, but here he has apparently assimilated the form of a Sicilian sun-king as vulture, for above his head is a solar arc with rays. Thalia wears on each wrist a serpentine bracelet. As mountain-nymph and serpent wearer, she is much closer to the Bronze Age great goddess than to the classical Muse, Thalia. This identity is also suggested by the two lilies in the field, a flower constantly associated with the great goddess in Minoan Crete. One lily has a spiral leaf to suggest her connection with the labyrinth. On the left is an altar which is more likely hers than Zeus' since she is being carried away from it. The olive-crowned boy on the right is probably one of the young initiates of her cult, an equivalent of the Cretan Curetes.

The mysterious elements of the icon are the two objects in the lower right corner. What are they? A. B. Cook interprets the upper one as a ball that Thalia has been playing with and the lower one as Thalia's basket, presumably a picnic basket.[6] But this is surely an error. The basket is decorated with a checker-pattern and four spirals. In the context of the myth, this certainly must mean that the basket is both a labyrinth and a womb. For we are told that Thalia, in the domain of the earth-goddess, brought forth a pair of twins, no doubt solar twins of the type we are so familiar with. The domain of the earth-goddess where the birth took place would therefore be in the labyrinth as womb. The solar twins, however, are always, in a sense, calendar-born as well as womb-born, since they represent the solar year. Accordingly, the four spirals on the basket stand for the labyrinth as calendar, signifying, as they do, the four-year half-cycle.

But what is the significance of the ball? It is certainly not a plaything. It looks very much like a ball of wound-up thread, for threads can be seen crossing each other on the surface and a remnant of unwound thread, the end, hangs below in a loop. Now if we recall the most famous of all labyrinth myths, that of Theseus and Ariadne, we will remember that Ariadne gave Theseus a ball of thread to help him find his way out of the maze of the Cretan labyrinth. Theseus tied the thread at the entrance of the labyrinth and unwound it until he found and slew the Minotaur within, and then followed the thread back again to the entrance. In the icon a ball of thread is shown directly over the labyrinth design and, indeed, threads are even shown as if leading in or out of the labyrinth at its base.

The literary myth of Thalia, of course, mentions nothing about a labyrinth or a ball of thread. These objects, therefore, cannot have the meaning given to them in the classical myth of Theseus and Ariadne. We need an interpretation of them consistent with the special context of the myth and the icon. The myth tells us about the birth of twins, and the icon shows us a labyrinth as a womb. In such a context, a thread emerging from the entrance of a womb can only be understood as a symbol of the umbilical cord at birth. And this must have been the original significance of some lost icon of a ball of thread and a labyrinth in conjunction with Theseus and Ariadne that was misinterpreted by mythographers who did not understand that the labyrinth was a symbol of the womb in the Bronze Age. The thread of Ariadne must have once meant the umbilical cord of the newborn sun-king, who is born from the labyrinth which is both the womb of the goddess and her solar-lunar calendar.

A terra cotta figurine of the goddess, which comes from Boeotia, provides some evidence from the archaic period (Figure 53). This bell-shaped goddess with an elongated neck has movable legs, and was apparently meant to be hung from the fruit-laden bough of a tree at a fertility ceremony. Robert Graves identifies her as Ariadne, calling attention to the mythic tradition that Ariadne hanged herself.[7] The original ceremony would have had no reference to Ariadne's death, for the goddess is immortal. It no doubt was intended to promote fruitfulness, the womb of Ariadne being the source of all life.

In this context let us look closely at Ariadne, who, of course, we know also as the Lady of the Labyrinth. First we may note that behind her right arm is a *labrys* or double axe, an appropriate symbol for the Lady of the Labyrinth. Below the double axe is an eight-legged swastika. The swastika is a sun symbol and this one has eight legs to represent the eight-year solar-lunar cycle. There are two more eight-legged swastikas above her breasts. But we also find two four-legged swastikas on her right arm to represent the

157

FIGURE 53. A terra-cotta Ariadne from Boeotia. Archaic period. Beneath her breasts is a labyrinth design flanked by two cranes holding threads in their beaks. *Louvre, Paris.*

four-year half-cycle. One turns clockwise while the other turns counterclockwise, to represent the spiral toward death and the counterspiral toward rebirth. It also echoes the way in which the Knossos calendar is read, alternating in direction in a four-year sequence. In each hand she holds a fertility bough, suggesting the bough from which she herself hangs, symbolic of fertility.

A pendant hanging from her necklace is between her breasts. The significance of its shape we should recognize at once. Its opposed concave crescent-ends represent the new moon and the old moon crescents. Here again, are the sisters who give birth to one another. Ariadne, as mistress of the labyrinth of the calendar, is a moon-goddess and this is her special symbol. Count the tassels hanging from this symbolic pendant and you will find there are exactly eleven, her number because there are eleven days discrepancy between lunar and solar years.

The most prominent symbol of all, however, is a great rectangle which covers the entire front of her body below her breasts. It is bordered by four concentric tracks which are schematically like the four day-tracks on the border of the Knossos fresco calendar. Within the border are two wavy lines and a lozenge-pattern. Surely this must be the labyrinth itself of which she is the mistress. And it is at once both solar-lunar calendar, as its four tracks indicate, and a womb as its position on her body tells us. And, of course, we also know from the riddle of the Sphinx that Boeotia had such a solar-lunar calendar.

One symbolic element remains. On either side of the labyrinth stand two cranes. As we know, the crane is the bird of Hermes, who carries off the old year and brings in the new. The cranes, which migrate twice yearly, are doubled to represent this seasonal death and rebirth of the sun-king. From the beak of each hangs a wavy thread. This is the thread of Ariadne, the umbilical cord, which the birth-bird, the crane or stork, quite appropriately holds.

Surprisingly, an equivalent of Ariadne's thread appears in an ancient Irish myth recorded around the eighth century A.D.[8] This pagan myth called "The Voyage of Bran," was, as the myth itself tells us, once recorded in the Celtic ogam script and is a part of Celtic bardic lore of far earlier date than the eighth century A.D. The hero of this myth is the semi-divine king, Bran, whom Robert Graves identifies with the Bronze Age Pelasgian hero, Phoroneus.[9] Graves writes, "The Bran cult seems . . . to have been imported from the Aegean," and he provides a considerable body of evidence to back this claim.[10]

The myth tells how a mysterious woman appeared to King Bran and offered him a bough from an apple tree. Thereupon she sang to him fifty quatrains about the silvery "Island of Women" from whence she had brought him the bough. This island is of a familiar type in mythology, being a happy land where none grow old, a version of the "isles of the blessed" or Ariadne's island of immortality. She urges Bran to set forth across the sea in a coracle in search of the Land of Women. He accepts the challenge and sails with a crew of thrice nine men, far to the west in the direction of the setting sun. After a prolonged voyage, which was not without peril, Bran finally approaches his goal.

The myth describes his arrival as follows:

> It was not long thereafter when they reached the Land of the Women. They saw the leader of the women at the port. Said the chief of the women: 'Come hither on land, O Bran son of Febal! Welcome is thy coming!' Bran did not venture to go on shore. The woman threw a ball of thread to Bran straight over his face. Bran put his hand on the ball, which adhered to his palm. The thread of the ball was in the woman's hand, and she pulled the coracle towards the port. Thereupon they went into a large house, in which was a bed for every couple, even thrice nine beds. The food that was put on every dish vanished not from them. It seemed a year to them that they were there,—it chanced to be many years. No savor was wanting to them.[11]

The myth continues relating how Bran eventually returned to Ireland.

This is certainly a familiar tale, despite the Celtic setting. It is one more variation on the labyrinth archetype, although a perilous sea voyage has been substitited for the

160

penetration of the labyrinth maze. The mysterious woman is obviously the great goddess who offers to her spouse, the sacred king, an apple bough symbolic of immortality. She is apparently a moon-goddess like Ariadne, for her song has fifty quatrains signifying the fifty lunations of the four-year half-cycle and she describes her island, which stands on four pillars, as "silvery," the moon's own color. The four pillars would correspond, incidentally, with the frame of the Knossos fresco calendar. Bran sets out with a crew of thrice nine men, which is twenty-seven and he himself makes the party come to twenty-eight, which is the number of days in a month in the ancient Celtic calendar. According to Robert Graves, the early Celtic calendar system had thirteen months of 28 days for a total of 364 days, with an extra day intercalated at the solstice each year for a grand total of 365 days.[12] This system, of course, is also compatible with a four-year solar-lunar half-cycle. Bran must also be a sun-king for he sails to the west, the direction of the setting sun.

Most interesting, however, is the description of his arrival at the island called the "Land of the Women." The chief of the women is surely the Lady of the Labyrinth herself. Now this is a myth of death and rebirth, for we are told that Bran, after a year, which was really many years, i.e. a great year, returned to Ireland, or in other words, was reborn. But his death is itself a spiritual rebirth, being a transcendence of death upon reaching the island of immortality. And how is he spiritually reborn? The chief of the women, a Celtic Ariadne, throws him a ball of thread by which she tows him to port in his coracle. Here is Ariadne's thread, the umbilical cord of birth once more. The coracle, of course, is a basket-like boat of woven reeds. We are already familiar with the basket as birth-vessel. The great house that Bran and his men enter is the womb of the goddess, where, appropriately, all twenty-eight are coupled and bedded signifying the sacred marriage, for just as in the Greek folk tale from Epirus, the sacred king seeks the goddess as both wife and mother.

The labyrinth as womb and calendar is symbolic of the sun-king's periodic birth, but also of his periodic death. The death aspect of the labyrinth calls for further illumination. The myth of Theseus slaying the Minotaur in the Labyrinth at Knossos may reflect, in some respects, an actual historical event—a tribute of seven youths and seven maidens demanded by the Mycenaean ruler of Knossos of the Athenians. With this aspect of the myth we need not here be concerned.[13] On the other hand, there are archetypal elements in the myth which are non-historical, some of which have already been noted. Theseus as slayer of the Minotaur is playing the part of an archetypal sun-king who ritually slays his twin at the summer solstice.

Let us look at an icon of Theseus slaying the Minotaur (Figure 54). It appears on a vase from Vari and dates from the sixth century B.C. On the left we see Theseus, sword in hand, holding the Minotaur by the horns. The Minotaur is being dragged from the Labyrinth which appears in the center of the picture. In each hand, the Minotaur holds a large round boulder. It is likely that these round objects in earlier icons were sun-disks, which were later interpreted as stones picked up by the Minotaur to defend himself. The Minotaur also has spots on his body, a detail we shall look into later. On the right of the Labyrinth stands Athena with her helmet and spear. She plays no part in the literary version of the myth, but her appearance here makes sense because she is the principal goddess of Athens, and Theseus is an Athenian hero.

In the late classical period, the Labyrinth of Knossos was usually considered a building with intricate passageways. And, as we have seen, the labyrinth as the tomb of a sacred king offers some justification for this view. But that is only one of its connotations and the evidence indicates that the labyrinth pictured as a building is a late conception in iconography. In this early sixth century blackfigured *lekythos,* the labyrinth is a rectangular panel bearing little resemblance to a building. On the panel, horizontal bands are painted with track-like marks above and below bands of sequent spirals, rather freely rendered. The panel has an overhanging lintel above and a threshold below, as if it were in a symbolic sense a doorway. In all these respects, it more nearly resembles features of the Knossos fresco calendar than a building. The calendar has track marks for counting days enclosing sequent moon-symbols and the border is rendered like a door, with a threshold below and an overhanging lintel above. To be sure, this labyrinth does not

162

FIGURE 54. A black-figured *lekythos* from Vari. Sixth century B.C. Theseus slaying the Minotaur. In the center, the Labyrinth. On the right is Athena connected to the Labyrinth and Theseus by a thread.

contain a bull-vaulting scene in the center, but after all that is inessential to the fresco as calendar. The border of the fresco is the labyrinth and that is what this icon emphasizes. It also emphasizes the doorway aspect of the labyrinth.

It is interesting that one ancient authority, in referring to the labyrinth, expressly mentions the lintel above the door. According to A. B. Cook, Pherekydes mentioned "*ton zygon tis ano Thyras*" or "the lintel above the door."[14] Cook does not explain why Pherekydes called attention to the lintel above the door to the labyrinth, probably because it is not clear from the context, but it appears that the door aspect of the labyrinth was important.

Other icons of the labyrinth on early pottery represent it as a flat panel with spiral or meander patterns in bands. And A. B. Cook writes, "the further back we trace the whole design, the more important becomes this particular feature of it."[15] One early black-figured piece recovered from the Acropolis at Athens among the debris left after the Persian invasion bears this out (Figure 55). In this version the labyrinth bears no resemblance to a building at all. It is simply a rectangular panel painted with C-spirals on horizontal bands. As such it suggests a fresco border with calendric symbols in bands.

FIGURE 55. A black-figured *skyphos* from the Acropolis at Athens. At the right, the Labyrinth is pictured as a rectangular panel banded with running spirals.

A later red-figured vase from Attica represents a transitional stage in labyrinth iconography (Figure 56). It shows Theseus dragging the Minotaur forth from a labyrinth, which is patterned with spirals and checker patterns. This is a remnant of calendric iconography. But there is also a doric column supporting an architrave at the entrance of this labyrinth, which reflects the tradition of the labyrinth as a building. The border design, however, is calendric in origin, since it is composed of running spirals divided by nine checker patterns for the ninth year of the solar king's reign.

FIGURE 56. Theseus and the Minotaur. The Labyrinth has a facade with a Doric column as well as checker and spiral patterns. *British Museum*.

Now let us return to the unexplained spots on the Minotaur pictured in Figure 54. A red-figured *kylix* from Vulci provides a clue (Figure 57). This damaged ceramic piece shows a figure in a short tunic about to slay a minotaur with a sword. Strangely enough, this minotaur's body is covered with eyes like Argos. As we know, Argos was himself originally a sun-king like the Cretan Minotaur and his eyes were sun symbols. It is therefore not inappropriate to equate one with the other. The spots on the Minotaur in Figure 54 were probably also intended to be sun symbols. An early sixth century B.C. ceramic piece from Corinth shows a minotaur surrounded by four eight-rayed sun symbols (Figure 58). Here the symbols are not on the minotaur's body, but his close association with them makes the same point, namely that he is a sun-king, whose proper number, of course, is eight.

FIGURE 57. A red-figured *kylix* from Vulci. The Minotaur is spotted with eyes like Argos. *British Museum.*

FIGURE 58. A Corinthian *pinax* from Pente Skouphia. Early sixth century B.C. The Minotaur surrounded by four eight-rayed sun symbols. *Berlin Museum.*

Still another variation on the spotted minotaur may be seen on a black-figured vase of later date (Figure 59). Here again the minotaur's body is spotted, but not with eyes, circles, or radiant symbols. The significance of these marks is problematical. They are shaped like the Greek letter T, pronounced in Greek *Tau*. I take them to signify the Greek word *Tauros,* meaning "bull." The *Minotaur* is, of course, the Minos-bull. Since there are exactly eight of these T's on the minotaur's body, we may confidently infer that they signify the eight-year cycle.

It is possible that a further significance was attached to the letter T. Lucian in his *Trial in the Court of Vowels* (c. 160 A.D.) writes:

> Men weep, and bewail their lot, and curse Cadmus with many curses for introducing *Tau* into the family of letters; they say it was his body that tyrants took for a model, his shape that they imitated, when they set up the erections on which men are crucified. *Stauros* the

FIGURE 59. A black-figured vase. A Minotaur marked
with eight T's.

· vile engine is called, and it derives its vile name from
him.[16]

Unfortunately Lucian does not tell us precisely how the T-
shaped gibbet derived the name *Stauros* from the letter *Tau*.
Obviously *Tau* is a syllable of *Stauros*. But it strikes me as
significant that the two syllables of the word give us *Tauros*
or "bull." The reason for the initial "S" remains a mystery.
But it seems a reasonable conjecture that the ritually sacrificed Minotaur was associated with the T-shaped cross,
upon which human sacrificial victims were crucified. In

Crete another type of the sacrificed sun-king, who was also associated with the bull, was Talos, whose name also begins with T.

We have seen that the archetype of the labyrinth has a birth aspect and in opposition to this, a death aspect. And we have also seen that the archetype resolves this dialectic of life and death in a third transcendent aspect. This transcendent aspect is most notably symbolized by the *labrys* or double axe from which the labyrinth takes its name. And this is no doubt why a tomb of the Late Minoan II period at Isopata in Crete was cut out in the form of a double axe. Sir Arthur Evans called this grave "the Tomb of the Double Axes" and he writes of it as follows:

> The cult of the dead is thus brought into direct relation with the divinity or divinities of the Double Axes, and we may infer that in the present tomb the mortal remains had been placed in some ceremonial manner under divine guardianship.[17]

To explore this aspect of the labyrinth further, we need to examine the *labrys* motif and some of its surprising connections. It has already been pointed out how the labyrinth motif of a quadrilateral with crossed diagonals was derived in Minoan Crete from a double axe placed between bull's horns or their equivalent, the altar pieces known as "horns of consecration," and how this pattern in turn relates to the calendar. But a further interesting development may be seen in those labyrinths which are primarily maze patterns.

The earliest of these maze patterns which has as yet come to light in an area where we might expect to find influence from Minoan Crete appears upon the reverse of a clay tablet from Pylos (PY Cn 1287).[18] This labyrinth from the Palace of Nestor can date no later than c. 1200 B.C. when the palace was destroyed by fire. It is therefore a genuine Bronze Age labyrinth of the maze type (Figure 60).

This labyrinth has been discussed by L. J. D. Richardson, who has convincingly demonstrated how the pattern can be drawn by a logical process of extension starting with the figure of a double axe. How this is achieved by a meander pattern dictated sequentially by the shape of the double axe may be seen in Figure 61. Richardson writes,

> To find that the double axe is capable of a metamorphosis, by projecting itself by means of a simple meander into the figure of the labyrinth, makes a *direct* association between *labrys* ('double axe') and *labyrinthos* ('the place of double axes').[19]

Richardson thinks that this design had become disassociated from religious connotations at Pylos and was used simply as a secular mason's mark. He writes,

> The labyrinth from Pylos, at its early date, may have been still consciously connected with the double axe, but, if so, probably no more than through the associations of the name *labyrinthos*.[20]

Whether or not the Pylian labyrinth had lost its original significance is a question which cannot be answered with any certainty. Our concern is rather with the question of whether this particular design *ever* had a religious significance.

Richardson points out that this labyrinth should be distinguished from other maze designs by its unvarying structure. It does not have any false alternative corridors in which one can get lost as, for instance, in the maze at Hampton Court. On the contrary, the passage leads from the entrance to the central *cella* with a grim inevitability. Furthermore, the number of turns is strictly determined by the double axe figure upon which it is oriented. This unvarying pattern can, therefore, be recognized in other contexts and particularly on Hellenistic coins of Knossos. Accordingly, Richardson calls it "The Labyrinth of Knossos" without, however, assuming any necessary connection with the far earlier Labyrinth of Minoan times.

Richardson also shows how this pattern can be rendered with curved rather than straight lines to form a circular labyrinth without changing its basic structural plan in the least. And he calls attention to the labyrinth on the Tragliatella *oinochoe*, which is a circular version of this type. We

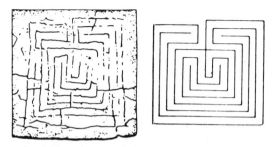

FIGURE 60. A clay tablet from Pylos (PY Cn 1287). The labyrinth as a maze. (c. 1200 B.C.)

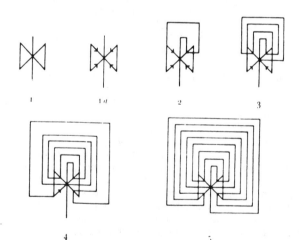

FIGURE 61. Diagram showing how the labyrinth of Pylos derives from the figure of the *labrys* or double axe. L.J.D. Richardson, "The Labyrinth", *Proceedings of the Cambridge Colloquium on Mycenaean Studies* (Cambridge, 1966), p. 291.

have already examined the iconography of this Etruscan wine jar, which dates more than five hundred years later than the Pylian labyrinth (Figure 13).

We have found that the icons on both sides of this *oinochoe* are decidedly of religious import, being representations of both ritual and calendric significance. Plainly, "the Labyrinth of Knossos" in this context is not a mason's mark. We have found it to be a symbol of the womb of the great goddess, as the small figure of the fetus testifies, as well as a symbol of the intricate mimetic dance called the Troy Dance. This, however, does not prove that the symbol had the same significance at King Nestor's palace in sandy Pylos. What the Tragliatella labyrinth *does* prove is that this design *once* had very important religious connotations, which may have been lost to the Greeks of Pylos of Nestor's time, while they were preserved by Etruscan religious tradition.

The Etruscan labyrinth appears in a calendric context. The Knossos fresco calendar, although also related in shape to the double axe, presents a different type of maze from that under discussion. Nevertheless, the two types have important things in common. Both are related to the shape of the double axe, but in both this relationship is not immediately apparent to the eye. Indeed, it appears that the *labrys* symbol has been deliberately concealed in the labyrinth, so as to be unapparent to all but the initiated.

Another similarity comes to light when one compares the route by which each labyrinth must be threaded in order to enter it and return. To reach the inner *cella* of the Pylos type of maze from the entrance, one must make eight circuits, counting the actual entrance to the *cella* as the last circuit, since here one must turn around to get out again. And in making these eight circuits, one must reverse directions alternately, clockwise and counterclockwise. Both these principles apply equally to the Knossos fresco calendar maze. To read the calendar for an eight-year cycle, one makes eight circuits alternating in direction with each successive circuit.

Richardson has shown that the shape of the double axe geometrically determines the shape of the Pylos-type maze and, consequently, its eight circuits. Therefore, the eight-circuit maze could not have been invented in direct imitation of the Knossos calendar maze. Their similarity, apart from the

172

double axe symbol, is mere coincidence. But, then, what a coincidence! To the Bronze Age draftsman doodling upon the sacred symbol of the double axe, the analogy would have appeared not a coincidence, but a revelation. The octopus with its eight spiraling tentacles radiating from a central body evolved through a process of natural selection. But that did not prevent the mythopoeic mind from projecting upon it by analogy, significance as a sun symbol. Hence, it is not unreasonable to suppose that the Knossos calendar maze and the Pylos type maze were at one time accepted as symbolic equivalents.

Maze-like labyrinths occur in other cultures beyond the area of our immediate concern. John W. Layard, drawing upon examples from the New Hebrides, southern India, and the Celtic sphere as well as Crete, summarizes what he considers to be the principal traits of the labyrinth as follows:

1. That it always has to do with death and rebirth relating either to a life after death or to the mysteries of initiation.

2. That it is almost always connected with a cave (or more rarely a constructed dwelling).

3. That in those caves where the ritual has been preserved the labyrinth itself, or a drawing of it, is invariably situated at the entrance to the cave or dwelling.

4. That the presiding personage, either mythical or actual, is always a woman.

5. That the labyrinth itself is walked through, or the labyrinth design walked over, by men.[21]

If we reflect upon the examples of the labyrinth archetype in the myths and icons which we have examined, we will see that these traits, in part or in concert, have indeed appeared again and again. It should also be obvious that the labyrinth archetype has its roots deep in the human psyche, regardless of what particular theory may most accurately explain, in part or in whole, the process by which it emerged or migrated, or was modified by differing cultural complexes.

The basic psychological significance of all examples of

this archetype, including those from beyond our area of concern, may perhaps by stated as follows. The labyrinth presents to the hero (the male human consciousness) a challenging quest. The hero is seeking a union with the feminine principle, in its broadest as well as its deepest sense. The young man of our folktale sought a wife, but also a mother. The sun-king seeks a union with the moon-goddess which permits him to know all her phases—as virgin, nymph, wife, mother, and as the hag, Hecate, his slayer. This quest for union with the feminine requires of the hero a perilous journey, which is represented by the maze aspect of the archetype. There is a very real psychic danger that he will lose his way or lack the fortitude to reach this desired union. In other words, he may fail the test of his initiation whether that be as a lover, a husband, a father, or a man facing death. It also means the test of the conscious ego which must maintain stability and sanity in regard to the powerful forces in the "underworld" of the unconscious. However, if the hero perseveres and reaches the central *cella* of the maze or the end of the eight-year cycle of the calendar maze, he unites with the principle he sought. The union, again, has many senses—the moment of conception in the womb where the sperm seeks the ovum, the moment of coordination of solar and lunar years, and the moment of the ego's acceptance of death. But in this supreme moment, all opposites are reconciled—male and female, sun and moon, space and time, life and death. Hence, this is the moment of transformation, of a death which is also a rebirth. This is the transcendent aspect of the labyrinth archetype, which by reconciling opposites becomes a mandala of wholeness. And this, as we have seen, is the function also, psychologically speaking, of Thrice Great Hermes, the hero in his transcendent state.

By a surprising transformance in the history of mythic archetypes, Thrice Great Hermes, disguised as the Three Wise Men of the East, comes to pay homage to the sun-king, Jesus, born of the ever virginal great goddess, then called "Mary," at his winter solstice birth. Three centuries later the Roman Emperor, Constantine, was converted to Christianity and adopted as his battle standard a symbol called in Latin the "labarum." This symbol takes its name from the "labrys" or double axe and it consists of the Greek letter X vertically transfixed by the Greek letter P to form the image of a hafted double axe expressed thus: ☓. In this form it becomes an emblem of Christ, being the first two consonants in his name.

Is this the sign which legend tells us Constantine saw in a dream? *In hoc signo vinces*—"In this sign shalt thou conquer!" Legend or no, in this sign Constantine, the first Christian Roman Emperor, did conquer, and to this day it may be found on countless Christian churches throughout Europe and America. The "labarum," as A. B. Cook pointed out long ago, was a Christian transformation of the ancient mystic symbol of the double axe.[22] Hence, Christ, the sun-king, appears in the *labrys* or, in other words, in the labyrinth. I hardly need remind the reader that in Christian iconography, Christ is equated with the lamb. And so, by a strange metamorphosis, the figure of the lamb, as Christ, appears as the lamb in the labyrinth as it did in the Greek folktale with which this chapter began.

CHAPTER IX

Come Seven Go Eleven

Oswald Spengler writes, "The origin of numbers resembles that of myth. Primitive man elevates indefinable nature-impressions (the 'alien,' in our terminology) into deities, *numina,* at the same time capturing and impounding them by a *name* which limits them."[1] When the name, however, was that of the supreme deity, it was frequently disguised both in respect to the letters which spelled it and their number. The ancient Hebrew name of God was not permitted to be spoken or written in full, but only in disguise as the Tetragrammaton, a four-letter formula made up of the consonants alone. The four-letter formula JHVH veiled the sacred name *Jehovah* both in respect to the secret vowels and the number of letters, which were seven in all. Seven was a number sacred to the deity, and, as everyone knows, the book of *Genesis* presents a myth of the creation of the world by God in seven days.

Similarly, the sun-god, Mithras, a god of Persian origin with many converts in the Roman legions of Imperial times, was signified by the formula name ABRAXAS because the true name of the deity was too holy to be spoken in a profane context. In *The Lost Language of Symbolism,* Harold Bayley writes,

> The name ABRAXAS, which is at the root of the famous magic-word Abracadabra, was one of the numerous

176

mystery words coined to express mathematically the unspeakable name of the Supreme Spirit. "Abraxas" was accepted as a mystic equivalent of "Mithras," because the numerical values of the two names both alike work out to the number 365.[2]

According to the *Oxford English Dictionary,* ABRAXAS was the name of the supreme god of the Gnostic sect of Basilides and its letters were symbolically equal to 365.[3] Evidently the Mithraic cult influenced the Gnostic sect for St. Irenaeus (c. 120–202 A.D.) in his *Adversus Haereses* confirms that the Gnostics considered the Greek letters spelling ABRAXAS to signify the number 365.[4]

There can be no doubt that the god, Mithras, and apparently also ABRAXAS, was associated with the solar year of 365 days. The birthday of Mithras was celebrated on December 25 because of the proximity of the winter solstice and, in fact, the early Christians adopted this date as the official birthday of Christ, by way of competing with the highly popular Mithraic cult. A stone altar-piece from a Mithraic shrine now in the Museum at Wiesbaden in Germany shows Mithras in conjunction with the twelve signs of the zodiac and joined with Sol, or the sun, and Luna, the moon.[5] The inference to be drawn is that the cult of Mithras may have had a solar-lunar ritual calendar. The number of letters in both the name Mithras and ABRAXAS is seven, which is also the sacred number of letters in the name, *Jehovah.*

The Latin word ABRACADABRA was derived from the Greek ABRAXAS.[6] The word consists of eleven letters which were sometimes arranged in a triangular pattern, in which the number of letters was diminished by one in each descending sequence. This permits the word to be read from left to right horizontally, or from the apex of the triangle to the base diagonally. When arranged in this way (Figure 62), the number of letters in the word as read on the base of the triangle amounts to eleven, but read again from the apex to the base we have eleven more or twenty-two letters, and the remaining side of the triangle has eleven again to make a total of thirty-three letters in all. In the solar-lunar calendar with which we are familiar, the number eleven is the number of days discrepancy between solar and lunar years which accumulates in three years to thirty-three and permits the intercalation of a month and makes the system work. Could it be that the word ABRACADABRA like AB-RAXAS is a formula concealing a calendar secret revealed only to initiates of the cult of Mithras?

```
A B R A C A D A B R A
A B R A C A D A B R
A B R A C A D A B
A B R A C A D A
A B R A C A D
A B R A C A
A B R A C
A B R A
A B R
A B
A
```

FIGURE 62. ABRACADABRA in triangular form as it frequently appeared as a charm on amulets.

It is curious that both ABRAXAS and AB-RACADABRA appear to allude to the normal sequence of the initial letters of the alphabet as arranged by the Greek Gnostics and given numercial significance. The sequence would appear to be A - B - X in the Greek, rendered as A - B - C in the Latin. The numbers seven and eleven which these names total, appear again in a context which is both alphabetic and calendric. I have in mind the ancient Etruscan alphabet which antedates the Gnostics by about nine hundred years.

The Etruscans had an alphabet (quite different from the Roman one), which derived twenty-two of its letters from north Semitic characters and an additional four from Greek characters. The Etruscans added one letter of their own, 8, which had the phonetic value of F. Their early alphabet, then, consisted of twenty-seven letters, twenty-two consonants and five vowels. Their *abecedaria* had a fixed order which was held to be sacred and probably concealed in formula religious and calendric secrets. That the alphabet contained sacred mysteries in formula is attested by the fact that they retained all twenty-seven letters in their *abecedaria* right down to the fifth century, although six of these letters were not used in practical communications because the sounds of their speech did not require them.[7] The explanation is probably that they were kept and learned for religious reasons.

By good fortune the standard order of the letters of the Etruscan alphabet has been preserved on an ivory writing tablet of the seventh century B.C.[8] No doubt the tablet was used to teach children their ABC's. The five vowels are placed in the sequence in what appears to be a deliberately designed order. A is in position 1, E in position 5, I in position 10, O in position 16, and U in position 23. The table in Figure 63 shows that the number of consonants between each succeeding vowel increases by one, i.e. 3, 4, 5, 6 consonants in order. The letter T is in position 22 and vowel 5 is in position 23. If vowel order and consonant order are counted separately, we would have 22 consonants ending with the letter 8, and the five vowels could be given an implied alternative position as the first or last five letters of the alphabet. We should also note that the letter in position 22 is followed by the last of the five vowels. The consonant in position 22 is T and the last of the five vowels is U. As it will later be shown, 22 and 5 are key numbers in the Etruscan calendar system. Their juxtaposition here could hardly be accidental. And it is probably also significant that T is the initial letter of the principal Etruscan God, *Tin,* while U is the initial letter of his spouse, the Goddess *Uni.* Their junction here combines the male solar number 22 with the female lunar number 5. It only remains to add that the letter R, which appears last in the sequence A-Bra-Ca-Dab-Ra is consonant 16. We shall see that this number is of primary importance in the Etruscan calendar system.

The Etruscan alphabet with its 22 consonants retained in formula, although some of them were never actually used, suggests that 22 may have been an Etruscan calendar number of significance. We may also recall that the Etruscan *oinochoe* discussed in Chapter II pictures on one side a ritual sacrifice of a sacred king who is to be dispatched by his tanist and escort with 22 spears. This wine jar, by the way,

No.	Cons.	Vowels	Etrusc.	Latin	Groups
1		1	𐌀	A	
2	1		𐌁	B	
3	2		𐌂	C	3 — 5
4	3		𐌃	D	
5		2	𐌄	E	
6	4		𐌅	V	
7	5		𐌆	Z	4
8	6		𐌇	H	
9	7		𐌈	TH	
10		3	𐌉	I	
11	8		𐌊	K	
12	9		𐌋	L	
13	10		𐌌	M	5
14	11		𐌍	N	
15	12		𐌎	S	
16		4	𐌏	O	
17	13		𐌐	P	
18	14		𐌑	S	
19	15		𐌒	Q	
20	16		𐌓	R	6
21	17		𐌔	S	
22	18		𐌕	T	
23		5	𐌖	U	
24	19		𐌗	KS	
25	20		𐌘	PH	5
26	21		𐌙	KH	
27	22		𐌚	F	

FIGURE 63. Table of Etruscan alphabet.

dates from the seventh century B.C. as determined by the archaic form of the Etruscan letters inscribed on it, and it is said to be one of the oldest painted ceramic works of local Etruscan manufacture.[9] Therefore, it reveals a very early Etruscan form of ritual probably regulated by the Etruscan calendar.

What was the structure of the early Etruscan calendar? Although a few scraps of information may be assembled from Roman and other sources, its fundamental principles remain unknown. The Etruscan language is still for the most part undeciphered. Perhaps when our knowledge of the language is perfected, extant inscriptions will reveal the Etruscan calendar structure in detail. Roman records show that a book once existed on the Etruscan measurement of time, but this book has not survived.[10] However, I believe it is possible to discover some of the working elements of the Etruscan calendar system with tolerable accuracy from evidence already available.

No doubt the city states of Etruria maintained calendars incorporating local variations in festivals as the state calendars of Greece did, but the twelve major Etruscan cities were united in a league primarily upon the basis of a common religion, and consequently we may expect that their calendar system was probably uniform in its structural elements. In an effort to discover what these structural elements are, let us begin by assembling whatever evidence we can find from various sources.

It is known that the Etruscan system had a lunar aspect, and that lunations were counted from new moon to new moon. Days were counted from noon to noon. This method differs from that of the Romans, who counted from midnight to midnight, and the Babylonians, who counted from dawn to dawn. The method has an advantage over the Babylonian system in that days are of equal length regardless of the season, and an advantage over the Roman system in that an accurate high noon may be found with an instrument no more complicated than a perpendicular rod or gnomon. A care to measure days and lunations accurately is indicated by these methods.[11]

They celebrated the day of new moon, the day of full moon, and the ninth day before the full moon. The day of full moon was called the *idus*, from which the Romans derived the *ides*, the fifteenth day of the month, and the *nones*, the ninth day before the *ides*. The word *calends*, the Roman name for the first day of the month, is not Etruscan, but the day of the new moon was certainly recognized in some way. Extant inscriptions permit the inference that two, at least, of their months known by name, *Acle* (June) and *Celius* (September) had thirty days. And the Latinized names of eight of their months have been preserved: *Velcitanus* (March), *Cabreas* (April), *Ampiles* (May), *Aclus* or *Acle* (June), *Traneus* (July), *Hermius* (August), *Celius* (September), and *Xosfer* (October).[12]

It is likely that the Etruscan year began with March, as the Roman year did. The New Year was probably related to the spring equinox, but not necessarily in precisely the same way as in the Roman calendar. There appears also to have been a five-day New Year festival which was not counted as a part of the official year, leaving 360 days for the official year, as in the Knossos calendar.[13] It may be inferred on the basis of one ancient authority (Macrobius: I, 13) that the Etruscan year originally consisted of only ten 30-day months, the equivalents of our January and February being omitted from the official year.[14] This would give a 300-day official year, rather than a 360-day year. But it is also known that a later Etruscan year counted twelve months.[15]

Obviously the Etruscan calendar had a lunar aspect. Did it have a solar aspect as well? Numerous icons of Etruscan make, which have already been discussed, point unmistakably toward rituals of solar kingship in relation to a moongoddess. From this evidence alone, one is led to expect a solar-lunar system of some kind.

A myth preserved from Roman times may offer a suggestive clue. The myth is told in connection with the Roman goddess of the New Year, Anna Perenna, whose name means "the year perennial." Her festival was celebrated on the fifteenth of March, five days separating it from the spring equinox. In Rome Mars was the young New Year god, after whom the first month was named. At this time of the year, it is related that the smith, Mamurius, made eleven moon-shields to counterfeit one actual moon-month.[16] Mamurius, since he was a smith, appears to be a Latin variation upon the Etruscan Velcitanus or Vulcan, who was also a smith and who gave his name to the Etruscan equivalent of March or the first month. In this context, the eleven moon-shields counterfeiting an actual month must certainly be interpreted as a number used in reconciling solar and lunar time, being the number of days discrepancy between a solar and lunar year.

A second clue is provided by Etruscan practice in haruspicy and augury. The Etruscan priesthood had an elaborate system of divination from the liver of a sacrificed animal, the practice called haruspicy, and of augury from observation of the flight of birds or the quarter from which lightning struck. A bronze model of a sheep's liver, found near Piacenza, is divided into sixteen compartments, each labeled with the name of the divinity presiding over it. This is a model that was used in teaching the practice of haruspicy. In discussing this model liver, Paul MacKendrick writes,

> The same sixteen subdivisions were used in the imaginary partition of the sky for augury, and the same principle governed the layout and orientation of cities like Marzabotto and probably Spina.[17]

The schematic layout for augury which parallels that of haruspicy may be seen in Figure 64. The priest would take up his position for augury in the center of the city facing south. The half of the city behind him would be the *pars postica* (posterior part) and the half before him, the *pars antica* (anterior part). On his left was the *pars familiaris* (lucky side) and on his right the *pars hostilis* (unlucky side). The quarter from which birds of omen appeared or lightning struck could then be interpreted in regard to the particular divinities ruling the sixteen divisions of the horizon.

Now this is a spatial system, but I suspect that it was a temporal system as well, since the 360-day year could be conveniently divided into sixteen parts corresponding to the solstices, the equinoxes, and four subdivisions of each quarter. This would seem sheer fancy if it were not for the fact that a number of the deities governing these segments correspond with the names of known Etruscan calendar months, or with Greek or Roman equivalent deities with calendric functions.

183

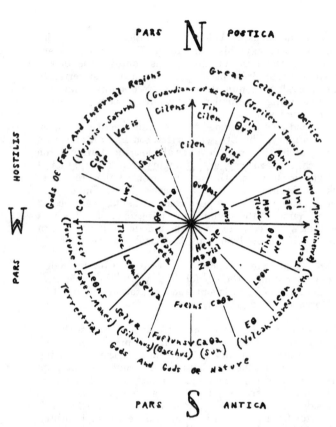

FIGURE 64. Etruscan sixteen-part division of the horizon for purposes of augury.

In the eastern half of this circle, we find *Mars* in the north quarter sharing honors with *Hercle* in the south quarter. Since *Mars* is associated with the spring equinox in Roman tradition, and since *Hercle* or Hercules has a month named after him in the Etruscan calendar, namely *Acle* (June), it is reasonable to suppose that the eastern half of the circle is divided by the spring equinox and that *Mars* and *Hercle* are solar twins of the archetypal kind. This would require that the western half of the circle be divided by the fall equinox. Here we find the northern quarter introduced by *Cel,* or the Latin *Celius,* after whom the Etruscan month of September is named as previously shown. The fall equinox falls, of course, in September.

Since June, as indicated by *Hercle,* appears in the southern half of the circle, the summer solstice should be located at this end of the vertical axis. The summer solstice is shared by *Fufluns,* known to be Bacchus, and *Catha,* known to be the Sun. They appear to be a second set of solar twins. Bacchus or Dionysus was, in fact, originally a sun-god. Even in the classical period, Dionysus shared honors at Delphi with Apollo, the sun-god, for a part of the solar year.

The northern end of the vertical axis would then have to be the winter solstice. Here *Cilens* occupies the western quarter, while *Tin Cilen* appears in the eastern quarter. Again it seems we have a pair of solar twins. Indeed, the two are shown to be in a sense two in one by the double name *Tin Cilen* and by the appearance of *Cilen* alone, repeated and placed so that the name spans the solstice line and, hence, pertains to both sides. As the diagram shows, they have been identified as "Guardians of the Gates." But this title has two senses. They are the gods guarding the gates of the city, which were ideally in the north in Etruscan cities, but they are also the guardians of the gates of the solar year, for the winter solstice is the gate through which the new year enters and the twins are its two pillars.

It is well known that *Tin* was the chief male divinity of the Etruscans and the Romans equated him with Jupiter, alias Zeus.[18] But this is misleading if one has in mind the late classical Jupiter or Zeus. *Tin* was attended by twelve *Dii Consentes,* meaning "Gods of Consent." These twelve were probably not originally independent Gods, but rather an Etruscan version of the archetype of the attendants upon a sacred king. *Cilens* has been identified with Hermes, who was born on Mount Cyllene in Arcadia, and gave the mountain its name.[19] Since *Cilens* and *Tin* are solar twins, we should expect to find a transcendent third, combining three in one. And so we do. The name *Cilen,* without an "s," ap-

185

pears on the diagram in the archetypal middle position between the twins, and written so as to span the solstice line, and, hence, combine the twins. In short, *Cilen* is an Etruscan equivalent of Thrice Great Hermes. It may also be seen from the diagram that *Tin* rules the celestial region, while *Cilens* rules the infernal region. This is appropriate since *Tin* is the waxing sun and *Cilens* is the waning or dying sun. And we may also recall that Hermes, alias *Cilens*, is the conductor of souls to the underworld or the infernal region.

The Piacenza liver, which parallels the diagram in its sixteen divisions, shows in a prominent central position a sun disk with a crescent moon inscribed. And on the convex side are inscribed the names *Usils* and *Tivs*, which have been identified by A. B. Cook as Etruscan for the "sun" and the "moon" respectively.[20] In the light of all the foregoing evidence and its consistency, I believe we may confidently infer that the number sixteen is calendric in significance. We have been searching for a clue to the solar aspect of the Etruscan calendar system. As an hypothesis, let us assume that sixteen refers to a partition of the 360-day solar year as the diagram (Figure 64) suggests.

Figure 65 is a diagram of the Etruscan year divided in this fashion. The official year is assumed to be 360 days, because there is reason to believe that a five-day festival at the New Year was considered outside of the official year. I shall assume that the year began at the spring equinox in accord with the evidence previously discussed. In fact, it makes little difference because the division of the year would work equally well in a mathematical sense from any starting point. If we divided the 360 days into sixteen equal parts, they would have 22.5 days each. This partition could be made in terms of whole numbers, if the periods were alternately 22 and 23 days in length. Since this makes possible a further subdivision, which there is reason to believe is sound, we shall accept it.

It is known as an historical fact that the Etruscans celebrated the first day of each month, the fifteenth day, the *idus* (*ides*), and the ninth day before the *idus*, called the *nones*. It is also known that they had an eight-day period known as an *ogdoad*.[21] If we begin at the spring equinox on the diagram (Figure 65), and subdivide the year by alternate

186

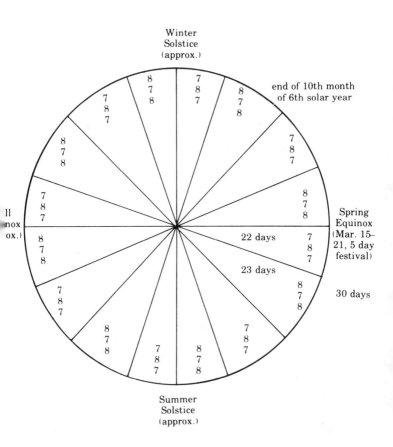

FIGURE 65. Diagram of the official Etruscan year of 360 days plus the 5-day festival which supplements this circle preceding the start of a new year at 21 March, as related to our more accurate year by year determinations of these stations of the solar cycle.

seven-day and eight-day periods, they will coincide with the alternate 22 and 23-day periods as well as with the divisions discussed above. The fifteenth day or *idus* will fall at the end of the second subdivision (seven days + eight days = fifteen days). The ninth day before the *idus,* the *nones* will fall on the last day of the first subdivision. The ancient Greek method of counting a sequence, and presumably also the Etruscan, included both the first and last terms, so that the ninth day by their count would yield what we would call the eighth.[22] Hence, the ninth day before the fifteenth would be the last day of the first subdivision. The end of the 30-day month would fall on the last day of the fourth subdivision (seven days + eight days + seven days + eight days = thirty days). The end of each sequence of three sub-divisions would coincide with the sixteen divisions of the solar year. Accordingly, we have a year of twelve 30-day months, forty-eight "weeks," and sixteen solar divisions. The perfect coordination of the known Etruscan subdivision of the month with the sixteen solar divisions confirms our hypothesis.

It would appear, then, that this is a solar-lunar system. The *idus* must have been celebrated because as the fifteenth day of a lunation, it would be the day of the full moon. But how would this sytem work in relation to the facts of solar-lunar astronomy? If we should begin a year with the ritual marriage of the moon-goddess and the sun-king at spring equinox, i.e. when a new moon happens to coincide with the equinox, when would these two meet again in accord with the system of twelve official 30-day months.

A synodic month or average lunation is approximately 29.53 days and a lunar year of twelve lunations is approximately 354.36 days. A solar year is approximately 365.25 days. Therefore, a lunar year is 10.89 days shorter than a solar year or in crude reckoning, 11 days shorter. How did the smith, Mamurius, make a counterfeit moon-month out of eleven moon-shields as the myth tells us? And what is the meaning of the report of Macrobius that the Etruscans once had only ten months in a year? We must answer these questions to fathom how the Etruscan system accounted for the discrepancy between official months and actual lunations, and official years and actual years.

Mathematical analysis shows that six lunar years or seventy-two lunations would terminate on the last day of the tenth official month of the sixth solar year, if we begin counting from a spring equinox which coincides with a new moon. We must also assume that the five-day New Year festival was lengthened to six days in the fourth year to account for leap year, all other divisions remaining constant. Six lunar years equals 2,126.16 days and six solar years equals 2,191.50 days. Therefore, in six years, the solar-lunar discrepancy, the eleven moon-shields, has built up to 65.34 days. If we subtract the five days of festival, which are not part of the official year, we get 60.34 days or a little over two 30-day official months. This six-year period is the shortest period in which it is possible to intercalate a period of 30 days or a multiple thereof, between the end of a true lunar year and the end of an official solar year of only 360 days, as designated by the system.

It is, of course, not a true solar-lunar cycle since new moon will not actually appear in the sky on the spring equinox, but about six days before it. Its function is rather to reconcile the official count of lunations with a true astronomical count. At the end of the tenth month of the sixth year, the official count of lunations is only seventy, whereas on precisely this day, the actual count is seventy-two. Therefore, two official extra months must be counted in addition to the two official months remaining in the calendar year, for a total of seventy-four lunations at the end of this six-year cycle.

These are the counterfeit months which Mamurius made of the eleven moon-shields. The myth no doubt speaks in poetic synecdoche, in saying Mamurius made one such month. If he made one, he could make two. And our ancient authority, Macrobius, appears to have been right in saying that the Etruscans had only ten months in a year. The sense is that after five regular twelve-month years, occurs a sixth year which ends with seventy-two lunations, the proper number, after only ten months. Furthermore, these are precisely the months, equivalent to our January and February, which it was inferred must have been dropped.

Now if we continue our count beyond the sixth year, the cycle can not repeat itself because, as we have seen, the new moon does not actually fall on the spring equinox and therefore we begin at a different point from our starting place before. However, it is simple to calculate how long a period must elapse before it will again be possible to insert one or more official 30-day months between the end of an actual lunar year and the end of the calendar year, without an inconsistent remainder. The shortest period which meets these requirements is five years, or eleven years from our original starting point.

Eleven lunar years equals 3,897.96 days, and eleven solar years, 4,017.75 days. The discrepancy is 119.79 days or very nearly 120 days. The first 60 of these days have already been accounted for at the end of the sixth year. Accordingly 60 days remain or two 30-day months, which may now be tallied at the end of the tenth month as a "counterfeit" addition to the official count. It should be noticed, however, that this time the two "counterfeit" months include the five-day festival, which was not true at the end of the six-year period. Hence, the lunar count ends exactly on the spring equinox. This reckoning again includes an extra day added to the New Year festival for leap year in the eighth year.

The eleven-year period like the six-year period does not make possible a perfect correlation of the new moon with the spring equinox. But it does approximate a correlation. The discrepancy would be about two days, figured on the basis of average lunations and a solar year of 365.25 days. Since the reckoning for a further count beyond eleven years begins on the spring equinox and since a new moon very closely approximates the equinox, it is possible to repeat the six-year cycle from this point without serious discrepancy. Thereafter the five-year cycle could be repeated bringing the count to twenty-two years. The system, then, would be based upon an eleven-year cycle, made up of alternating six and five-year periods.

Over a long period of time, the discrepancies we have noted would accumulate and become serious. It would then become necessary to begin afresh on the basis of an empirically determined coincidence of new moon and the spring equinox. But when would this adjustment have been made? There is solid evidence that this adjustment was made every 110 years. The 110-year cycle was known to the Romans who took it over from the Etruscans.

Robert Graves writes,

> The 110 years were made up of twenty-two Etruscan
> *lustra* of five years each; and 110 years composed the
> "cycle" taken over from the Etruscans by the Romans.
> At the end of each cycle they corrected irregularities in
> the solar calendar by intercalation and held Saecular
> Games.[23]

Graves, however, does not explain why the Etruscans
chose 110 years as a cycle, except to remark that it was the
product of 22 × 5, and that 22 was a sacred number because
it appears in the ratio *pi* or 22/7. A knowledge of the Etruscan calendar system provides a more satisfactory explanation. The 110-year cycle is ten times the eleven year cycle,
which is composed of alternating periods of six and five
years. Ten was probably chosen as the proper number by
which to multiply the eleven-year cycle because in a system
of counting based upon ten digits, the tenth is the crucial
one where the system repeats itself by beginning with
eleven. The 110 years are, therefore, literally a "century" of
eleven-year cycles.

The multiplication of 22 by 5, however, *is* symbolic because the combination implies significant calendric numbers.
The 22 implies the solar division of the year into sixteen
periods of alternately 22 and 23 days, while the 5 implies the
alternating cycle of five and six years. The 22 also implies a
repetition of that very important calendric number, 11. And,
finally, the product of 5 times 22 is 110, which is the century
number. The numbers 5 and 22 make a symbolic formula of
calendar secrets which appear to have been deliberately hidden, but preserved in the symbolism of the Etruscan alphabet.

If we now return to the table of the Etruscan alphabet
(Figure 63), it will not be difficult to see why the letters
were arranged in this particular sequence and learned by
every schoolboy. Why does the vowel A appear in position
one, while the second vowel E appears in position five? Because the 360-day official year begins and ends with a five-
day festival to make a total of 365 days. The last vowel U
appears in the fifth position from the end of the alphabet for
the same reason. These five days are sacred to the sun and

the moon and are represented by the five vowels, A, E, I, O, and U, which should be numbered separately. Why does the vowel I appear in position ten? Because juxtaposed to the consonant K, which is in position eleven, the century number 110 or 10 × 11 is indicated. Why does the vowel O appear in position 16? To indicate the 16 divisions of the 360-day year. Why does the vowel U appear in position 23? There are several reasons. First, because juxtaposed to the consonant T in position 22, an indication is given of the 16 alternate 22 and 23-day periods of the year. Secondly, because T and U in conjunction stands for the solar-lunar marriage of *Tin* and *Uni*. Thirdly, because the juxtaposition of vowel five with letter position 22 or T again produces the century number 110, or 5 × 22. Lastly, the vowel U appears five positions before the end to indicate the five-day festival which both begins and ends the year.

We may recall that the only character of the alphabet which the Etruscans themselves invented or adopted was 8 for F. Why did they choose this shape and place it at the last position in the series? Because this figure-of-eight design symbolically represents the fact that the calendar system repeats itself in a circle of eternal return.

I have ventured to suggest that the magic-word *abracadabra* contained a formula for alphabetic and calendar secrets known to the Greek Gnostics and derived from Mithraism. The letter R, which appears in both *abraxas* and *abracadabra,* is consonant number sixteen in the Etruscan alphabet and symbolizes the sixteen-part solar year. Could a Mithraic solar-lunar calendar have had a similarly divided year? But let us look further. If one examines again the triangular arrangement of *abracadabra* illustrated in Figure 62, one finds that the total number of letters is sixty-six. It happens that the total number of moon-shields, or days, that Mamurius, the smith, combined to make an intercalation at the end of the six-year Etruscan cycle was sixty-six or six times the eleven-day discrepancy. And it is also notable that *abracadabra* is composed of six consonants and five vowels, which would be a convenient way to indicate symbolically the secret of an alternation of six and five year periods in an eleven-year cycle. Of course, these correspondences may be sheer coincidence, but a Mithraic calendar parallel in structure to the Etruscan calendar is not unlikely. It is quite possible that the Etruscan calendar and the hypothesized Mithraic calendar may have had a common ancestor in Asia Minor and the Aegean in the Bronze Age.

The expression "Come seven, go eleven" stems from a game of dice in which seven is a lucky throw and eleven, unlucky. Where or when this game originated I do not know. But it is surprising how very ancient is the custom of playing games with dice. That the early Etruscans played at dice is certain, for a pair of dice marked with Etruscan letters signifying numerals was found at Tuscania.[24] There is also a legend reported by Herodotus about the Etruscans playing at dice. Herodotus tells us that the Etruscans, whom the Greeks called Tyrsenoi, were originally from Lydia. He says that after the Trojan War, they were affected by a severe famine. To conserve food, they adopted the system of eating only every other day and distracted their hunger on the alternate days by playing games of dice. This they did for eighteen years. Then since the famine was not abated, their king divided his people in half by drawn lots, and half remained with him while the other half under his son, Tyrsenos, set sail for another land and came eventually to Italy.[25]

The ancient Egyptians also played dice games, and apparently sometimes used a graduated board upon which counters were moved after each throw, for boards for playing draughts in this way have been found.[26] According to an Egyptian myth, the game of draughts had a connection with the Egyptian calendar. The Egyptian calendar appears to have been revised at one time for religious reasons. The revision involved the substitution of a 360-day year made up of twelve 30-day months, plus five days of festival for an older system of thirteen 28-day months, making a total year of 364 days, plus one festival day.

Describing this myth and its relation to the calendar, Robert Graves writes,

> The Egyptians said that the five days were those which the God Thoth (Hermes or Mercury) won at draughts from the Moon-goddess Isis, composed of the seventy-second parts of every day in the year; and the birthdays of Osiris, Horus, Set, Isis, and Nephthys were cele-

brated on them in this order. The mythic sense of the legend is that a change of religion necessitated a change of calendar: that the old Moon-goddess year of 364 days with one day over was succeeded by a year of 360 days with five over. . . . "[27]

The mathematics of this is very simple. If Thoth won the seventy-second part of each of 360 days, he won 360/72 or five days.

Now it is well established, on the basis of evidence from both Egypt and Crete, that the Minoans had close trade and cultural relations with ancient Egypt. According to J. D. S. Pendlebury, the cultural relations between Crete and Egypt were especially close in the Egyptian XII Dynasty (c. 1991– 1786 B.C.) or in Minoan chronology, Middle Minoan IIa and IIb.[28] This is interesting, because a Minoan gaming board of Middle Minoan date was found in the Palace at Knossos, and Stylianou Alexiou, describing it in the catalog of the Archaeological Museum of Heraclion, writes, "Similar draught-boards have been found in Egypt."[29] The Minoan board is dated somewhat later than the Egyptian XII Dynasty in Middle Minoan IIIb.

This game, like the Egyptian game, appears to have been played with dice and counters moved upon the board. Four counters made of ivory, which exactly fit certain round medallions on the board, were found near by, but in a slightly earlier deposit (MM IIIa).[30] Dice were not found here, but in the Palace at Phaistos a dice-box with a die in it was found in a Middle Minoan deposit. R. W. Hutchinson describes this find as a

dice-box in terracotta, containing what appears to be a die in the form of a small ivory disc with the numbers indicated by inlaid silver dots, as well as two possible "chess pawns," in the form of a small lion's head and an ox's hoof, in ivory.[31]

This find, by the way, is of slightly earlier date than the board, being Middle Minoan IIa (c. 1850–1780 B.C.).

I have closely inspected this gaming board and the four counters in the Heraclion Museum and have come to the

194

conclusion that the game played upon it was based on calendric numbers. Fortunately, it was found, as Pendlebury remarks, in a state so "well preserved to admit of certainty in its repair."[32] Consequently, an analysis of its mathematical elements stands upon a firm foundation.

The framework of the board is ivory which is inlayed with rock crystal, silver, gold leaf, and blue paste details to indicate the course of the game pieces or counters. An accurate drawing of it may be seen in Figure 66.

There it may be seen that the border consists of seventy-two sun symbols, each having exactly sixteen rays. We may recall that Thoth (Hermes) played the Moon-goddess, Isis, at draughts to win the seventy-second part of each of 360 days.

We may also recall that the Etruscan calendar had 16 solar divisions. The number of sun symbols on the two shorter sides equals 28, with 14 on each side. The remaining symbols between on the longer sides amount to 44, with 22 on each side. Are these not familiar numbers? The moon-month which Isis championed was 28 days, corresponding with the two shorter sides, while the solar division of the year, which Thoth apparently championed, was, it seems, 16 divisions of 22 and 23 days alternately, corresponding with the longer side. It certainly looks as if this is the game, or one much like it, which Isis played with Thoth in Egypt, and which may very well have passed from Egypt to Minoan Crete sometime in the XII Dynasty.

But how would the game be played? If it were not for the clue provided by calendric symbolism in conjunction with the Egyptian calendar myth, any attempt to interpret how the game was played would be hopelessly conjectural and doubtful. But with the help of these clues, I believe the riddle of this Sphinx, possibly an Egyptian Sphinx, may be solved.

It is reasonable to assume that the game was played by moving the pieces along the board a certain number of positions, as determined by each throw of a set of dice. The discovery of a dice-box and die at Phaistos of approximately contemporary date makes this a reasonable assumption. But at which end of the board should this movement begin? Since the eight bars at the left-hand end of the frame proceed from

195

FIGURE 66. Game board from Knossos. (c. 1600 B.C.) *Heraklion Museum*.

an open end like an entrance, while the four large medallions at the opposite end are boxed in by the frame, it is logical to assume that the game begins on the left side of the board.

The four ivory playing pieces found at Knossos fit the board positions neatly. They are approximately conical in shape, but if one inspects them closely, one finds that each has eight facets. Two have a larger diameter than the other two and one of the larger has three incised lines running around its base. I take the smaller two to represent the moon and the larger two, the sun. The diameter of the larger ones fits the diameter of the ten medallions adjoining the eight entrance bars, while the diameter of the smaller ones corresponds to the diameter of the inner circles on these medallions. All four pieces fit neatly into the space provided by the shorter side of the board, if the two moon-pieces are placed on the first two medallions, and the sun-pieces are placed side by side on the first bar of the eight at the entrance. A symbolic justification for this arrangement is that the eight bars are separated by lines of gold, the sun's color, while the medallions are blue and white, which are moon colors.

By this arrangement, which permits all four pieces to begin together, we can see that the course of moves to be made by the sun-pieces will differ from the course of the moon-pieces. What we should expect to find, if the game is the same as the one Thoth played with Isis, is that the course run by the moon should include 28 moves to correspond with the 28-day month.

Let us see if a 28-move course is detectable on the board beginning at the position chosen, and without any arbitrary use of the sequent positions. The course of a single moon-piece, let us say the one beginning in the lower left corner of the board, would logically be five moves on the five medallions, then four moves on the white bars beside the last medallion. Next there are six moves on the large bars in the center of the board. Then four more moves on the white bars at the lower right of the large bars just traversed. Next come the four large medallions, which are arranged in a sequence approximating a circle. Taking a hint from the counter-clockwise spiral at the lower right corner of the board, let us move to the nearest medallion on the right and move counter-clockwise about the circle of medallions, which will bring us back to the first medallion in five moves. There now remains only one logical place for the moon-piece to go, namely the position marked by the spiral in the lower right-hand corner of the board. But to use all available positions, let us move in sequence to the top right-hand corner spiral position and complete a course of the entire board. This comes to four more moves. Now let us tally the total number of moves. The count is 5 + 4 + 6 + 4 + 5 + 4 which equals 28 moves.

The game which Thoth and Isis played involved the days of the entire year. So far we have seen only the moves for one month of 28 days. The moon has 13 such laps to run on the board, if Isis is to win. The alternating directions of the spirals just traversed tell us that we must begin the next lap by reversing direction, so our first move will be from the clockwise spiral at the top corner of the board to a starting place on the counterclockwise spiral at the lower corner of the board. In four moves, we will return to the spiral at the top corner. Then we must move to the top large medallion and circle the medallions counterclockwise to return to the top medallion in five moves. Then we shall be in position to repeat the same sequence of moves as in the first lap, but this time on the upper side of the board, making thereby a loop. The count will be the same, 28 moves, but the moon-piece will wind up on the small medallion, on the opposite side of the board from which it began. The first move of the third lap will bring the piece back to the side on which it began, and a second loop may be made in twice 28 moves and so forth until 13 laps have been completed. But since 13 laps is an odd number, the moon-piece will wind up on the opposite end of the board, from the end on which it began. It will rest on the clockwise spiral at the upper right-hand corner of the board. The count will now be 364 moves. A single move to the counterclockwise spiral just below it for the single festival day of the year will bring the count to 365 moves and complete the game.

How would the sun run its race with the moon? We should expect to find that the sun-piece makes 16 laps of alternately 23 and 22 moves each. Let us see if this can be done from the given starting position, without an arbitrary

198

use of the positions on the board. There is room for two sun-pieces on the eight entrance bars, but let us follow the logical course of the lower one alone. Obviously the first eight moves are indicated by the eight bars. Then we must use the small medallions, but only those on the lower side of the board. That will amount to five more moves. Next we find six moves on the large bars on the center of the board. We have now reached the four large medallions. Whereas the course of the moon-piece was, consistent with its starting position, a sequence utilizing a marginal path on the board, the sun-piece, consistent with its starting position, has utilized the available central path on the board. Therefore let us move next to the nearest central large medallion, then to the lower one, then, in circular fashion, to the other central one, and finally to the upper one. The count is four more moves. Now we may tally the moves for a single lap, since we have used every position on the board in a sequence logically available to the sun-piece. The sun-piece, which precisely fits the diameter of the larger circle of the small medallions which both the sun and moon-pieces occupy, is too large in diameter to fit the positions indicated by the spirals. Only the moon-piece fits these positions. Hence, the circle of large medallions must complete a lap for the sun-piece. The tally for the lap is 8 + 5 + 6 + 4 which equals 23 moves.

In completing the first lap, we circled into the last position. To be consistent we should reverse directions and circle out again. This will mean only three moves, since we already occupy a position on one of the four medallions. In keeping with the looping course of the moon-piece, the sun-piece should also return on the opposite, but inner side of the board. Next is a sequence of six moves on the large bars. Then there are five moves on the upper five small medallions, and finally eight moves on the upper lane of the eight small bars. The total count in this lap is only 22 moves (3 + 6 + 5 + 8 = 22), because we already occupied one position on the last move of the first lap. Now we may begin the third lap by moving into the lower lane of the eight entrance bars, as the first of eight moves and the third lap will, like the first, take 23 moves. Hence, the logical use of all of the available sun-positions on the board demands alternate laps of 23 and 22 moves. The sun-piece must complete 16 of such laps on alternate sides of the board, for a total of 360 moves. Since 16 is an even number, the sun-piece, unlike the moon-piece, will wind up at the end of the board at which it began, but on the upper rather than the lower lane of the eight small bars. There will then remain five more moves on the upper five small medallions, and the sun-piece will come to rest on the last, having completed the game in 365 moves.

These last five moves are the five days that Thoth won from Isis. And we know from the myth that they constituted a five-day festival celebrating the birthdays of Osiris, Horus, and Set, the male trinity, represented on the board by the three small medallions on the uppermost level, while the two lower level medallions represent the birthdays of Isis and Nephthys, the pair of feminine deities. Finally, the seventy-two sun symbols on the border of the board represent the seventy-second parts of each day of the year, which were combined to make up the five festival days. A schematic diagram showing how the game may be played is provided in Figure 67.

Perhaps Thoth and Isis played the game with only one counter each, the winner being the one whose piece first reached home, i.e. the extra day for the moon-piece of Isis or the extra five days for the sun-piece of Thoth. But it would also be possible to play the game with four pieces, two moon-pieces for Isis and two sun-pieces for Thoth. It would then be necessary to get both pieces home to win.

This would be a more interesting game. Notice that on some parts of the board, both moon and sun counters use the same positions but on other parts they are either entirely separate, or there is room to pass in separate lanes without collision. Obviously, the greatest hazard of the game is in finding one's path obstructed temporarily by an opponent's piece. This would be simply a matter of chance if the game is played with one piece each, since it would be necessary for the obstructing opponent to move on the next throw and eventually clear the way. But if the game were played with two pieces each, it would be possible to choose which piece to move on each throw. Then an element of skill would be involved, for a player could choose to obstruct or not to obstruct his opponent, whichever would be to his greater ad-

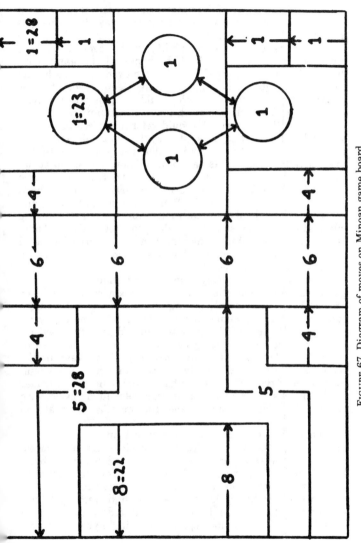

FIGURE 67. Diagram of moves on Minoan game board.

vantage. Since a set of four matched counters was found at Knossos, it seems likely that this is the way the game was played.

There is one more possibility to be considered. The Egyptian myth tells us that Thoth played the game with Isis, and in Crete it could have been played at times by the king and the queen. It might also have been played at times by two men, in which case it would be symbolically more appropriate for each player to move one sun-piece and one moon-piece. The player who could get both pieces home first would be the winner. Now it may be that the game was played merely as an amusement, but the possibility that it may have been played as part of a religious ritual ought not to be ignored.[33] We may recall that the two ivory game pieces found at Phaistos were in the form of a lion's head and an ox's (bull's?) hoof. In Minoan religion, the bull and the lion were calendar totem beasts representing the waxing sun and the waning sun of the solar year, respectively. There is, at least, a possibility that the game was part of a ritual celebration at the summer solstice, when the bull season gives way to the lion season.

This possibility brings up the question whether the game had any connection with the Minoan ritual calendar, or whether it was simply an import from Egypt reflecting a foreign calendar system. This question can not be easily resolved. A 360-day official year terminated by a five-day festival coincides with the system apparent in the Knossos fresco calendar. But the lunar division of the year in the Knossos calendar is definitely not the one which Isis championed in Egypt. On the contrary, the Knossos calendar works on the basis of an eight-year solar-lunar cycle with three intercalated months, and the months alternate in length.

There is one bit of symbolic evidence on the ivory game pieces which may be significant. Each piece has eight facets and one of the sun-pieces has three incised lines at the base. It is possible that the eight facets symbolize the eight-year cycle and the three bands stand for the three necessary intercalations of this cycle. Neither the eight-year cycle nor the intercalation system have any thing to do with the game as it is played. The game represents a single year only, and

202

the lunar divisions are foreign to the Knossos calendar system.

It must also be kept in mind that the gaming board is dated Middle Minoan IIIb or c. 1600–1500 B.C. Sir Arthur Evans dated the Knossos fresco Late Minoan I or c. 1500 B.C. Therefore it is uncertain whether the board and the fresco were nearly contemporary or separated by as much as a century. As for the Egyptian myth, there is no way of knowing its antiquity. The Egyptian gaming boards reported to be similar to the Knossos board by both Stylianou Alexiou and R. W. Hutchinson are, unfortunately, not available to me for study. Neither of these authorities mention the probable date of the Egyptian boards.

I think there need be no doubt that the Knossos board was made in Crete, for its artistic style is not Egyptian but characteristically Minoan, some of the motifs being like those found on Minoan pottery. On the other hand, this type of game may have been Egyptian in origin. On the basis of the evidence presently available, it is impossible to be sure. Nor can we be sure how it came about that the calendar in use in Etruria about the seventh century B.C. divided the solar year in a way that resembles the solar division in the game. It may have been independently arrived at by the Etruscans, or it may have been a Bronze Age heritage, brought with them from the Aegean to Italy. What we may be sure of is that the Knossos game is calendric in its numerical symbolism, and that it is related to the myth told of Thoth and Isis in Egypt. And we might add, indulging in a bit of poetic license, that the game is a game of sevens and elevens, since four throws of seven wins a lap for Isis and two throws of eleven wins a lap for Thoth.

We have now solved a number of riddles posed by the Sphinx and her relatives. And a number of her questions have been a question of numbers. It also appears that these numbers are in themselves archetypal and related mythically as well as mathematically. Dr. Marie-Louise von Franz, a Jungian psychologist, writes that

> the natural numbers—viewed from a psychological angle—must certainly be archetypal representations, for we are forced to think about them in certain definite

ways. Nobody, for instance, can deny that two is the only existing even primary number, even if he has never thought about it consciously before. In other words, numbers are not concepts consciously invented by men for purposes of calculation: They are spontaneous and outonomous products of the unconscious—as are other archetypal symbols.[34]

Viewed in the mythic context we have explored, these archetypal numbers emerge from the primordial One in an organically related process much like cell division. The Sphinx is the One who includes the Many. And this is a riddle indeed, for the entire history of philosophy consists of variant ways of solving the problem of the relation of the One to the Many. From her oneness emerges the archetypal twins, a division into Two of the Swan's egg of Leda. From the twin heroes arises the Third, the mysterious Thrice Great Hermes, the high-flying crane and earth-dwelling serpent who reunites the twins as well as the upper and lower world with the One as the archetype of the transcendent third.

The process continues for the first law of the Sphinx is to increase and multiply. Out of the Three comes the Four as an archetypal quaternity symbolized by the quadrangular labyrinth which spatially represents the four quarters of the horizon, and temporally represents the four seasons of the calendar year. Consequently four fabulous beasts are born—the bull, the lion, and the two serpents of Minoan calendric symbolism. A spatial variant on the archetype appears in a Christian context as the four evangelists, St. Luke, the ox, in one quarter, St. Mark, the lion, in the second, St. Matthew, the cherub, in the third, and St. John, the eagle, in the fourth, as they invariably appear marking the four cardinal points in early Christian basilicas.

The archetypal Five is contained in the labyrinth motif, for it is represented by the midpoint in the quadralateral where the crossed diagonals meet. It, too, appears in Christian symbolism, as the five wounds of Christ crucified on the four points of the cross. The archetype of Five appears in a variant form as the five Dactyls who emerge from the upheld hand of the goddess, or from both hands becoming ten attendants upon the sacred king. The ten in turn become an archetypal band of twelve by the addition of the twin kings. Hence we have the twelve Titans, the twelve Olympian Gods, and later the twelve apostles of Christ.

The first law of the Sphinx is to increase and multiply, but her second law is dissolution and death or a return to the One. So when the number Ten is reached, the archetype of completion or perfection, there is nowhere to go except back to the One. Consequently the number Eleven and its multiples represents death and rebirth, for both in the decimal system and in the solar-lunar calendar, it spells an end which is also a beginning. It is the archetype of the circle of eternal return, and as such, it appears as an element of the nuclear archetype, the labyrinth, around which all the other archetypes constellate. The labyrinth, then, with the Sphinx as its guardian, is the master archetype, the womb from which all things emerge and the tomb to which all things return. Just as the Sphinx is the One which contains the Many, the labyrinth is the Many integrated as the One. It unites all numbers, all archetypes as a mandala of wholeness, the alpha and omega, the first and the last.

Notes

INTRODUCTION

1. Robert Graves, *The Greek Myths* (Middlesex, England: Penguin Books, Ltd., 1969), I, p. 22.

CHAPTER I

1. Ecclesiastes, III, 1-8.
2. Alexander Marshack, *The Roots of Civilization* (New York: McGraw-Hill, 1972), *passim*.
3. Tons Brunés, *The Secrets of Ancient Geometry* (Copenhagen: Rhodos, 1967), vol. I, p. 27.
4. Evelyn Hutchinson, "Long Meg Reconsidered," I and II, *American Scientist*, vol. 60, no. 1 and 2, Jan.-Feb. and Mar.-April, 1972. This is an article reviewing the conclusions reached by Professor Thom which appeared in various publications.

The recently discovered need to recalibrate carbon 14 dating with the aid of dendrochronology (tree-ring dating) might call for a revision of the solar alignments to earlier dates.

5. Gerald S. Hawkins, *Stonehenge Decoded* (New York: Dell Publishing Co., 1965), *passim*.
6. Diodorus Siculus, *Works,* trans. C. H. Oldfather, vol. II (London: Harvard University Press, 1961), pp. 37–41; quotation from Hecataeus.
7. Martin P. Nilsson, *Primitive Time-Reckoning* (Lund: C. W. K. Gleerup, 1920), pp. 345–346.
8. Robert Graves, *The White Goddess* (New York: Random House, 1948), p. 297.
9. Graves, *White Goddess,* p. 459.
10. Nilsson, p. 363.
11. Robert Graves, *Greek Myths* (Middlesex, England: Penguin Books Ltd., 1960), vol. I, p. 22.
12. Michael Ventris and John Chadwick, *Documents in Mycenaean Greek,* Second Edition (Cambridge: Cambridge University Press, 1973), p. 303.
13. Ventris and Chadwick, p. 114.

Chapter II

1. For the evidence supporting the identification of the bull with the waxing year, and for a more detailed discussion of the ritual scene in general, see *The Thread of Ariadne* (New York: Philosophical Library, 1972), Chapter IX.

2. For a detailed discussion of the lion as the calendar beast of the summer season, see *The Thread of Ariadne,* Chapter VI.

3. Graves, *Greek Myths,* I, pp. 39–40.

4. V. E. G. Kenna, remarking on the high frequency of the spiral motif on Minoan seals, lists 104 seals featuring it and classified as to types. V. E. G. Kenna, *Cretan Seals* (Oxford: Oxford University Press, 1960), Appendix II, p. 31.

5. Herbert Westren Turnbull, "The Great Mathematicians," *The World of Mathematics,* ed. James R. Newman (New York: Simon and Schuster, 1956), p. 83.

6. H. L. Jones, trans., *The Geography of Strabo* (Cambridge, Mass.: Harvard University Press, 1961), VIII, pp. 103–107.

7. Jones, *Strabo,* VIII, p. 105, note 1.

8. Jones, *Strabo,* IV, p. 153.

9. Graves, *Greek Myths,* I, p. 318.

10. Vergil, *Aeneid,* trans. W. F. Jackson Knight (Harmondsworth, England: Penguin Books Ltd., 1968), pp. 147–148.

11. Emily Vermeule, *Greece in the Bronze Age* (Chicago: University of Chicago Press, 1960), p. 293.

12. Homer, *The Iliad,* trans. Sir William Marris (Oxford: Oxford University Press, 1934), pp. 430–431.

13. R. F. Willetts, *Cretan Cults and Festivals* (New York: Barnes and Noble, 1962) p. 124; quotation from Lucian.

14. Vergil, *Aeneid,* p. 137.

15. Graves, *Greek Myths,* I, pp. 297–298.

16. Graves, *Greek Myths,* I, p. 52 and p. 312.

17. The iconography of both sides of this wine jar has been given a somewhat different interpretation by Robert Graves. In the main, I agree with his interpretation, but differ with him in some important respects. He interprets the fetal figure as a "death-demon" and hence fails to see the significance of the labyrinth as a womb. This, of course, is my major point. See Graves, *Greek Myths,* I, p. 346 and p. 370.

18. Donald Strong, *The Early Etruscans* (New York: G. P. Putnam's Sons, 1968), pp. 20–26.

Chapter III

1. Graves, *Greek Myths,* II, p. 10.

2. More exactly the Phoenix cycle in Egypt was 1,460 years, because a year is longer than 365 days by 365/1460 days. In 1,460 years, a Sothic year, this fraction accumulated amounts to 365 days or one whole year. Jones, *Strabo,* VIII, p. 125.

3. This is not to say that Sophocles and Freud were "wrong" about Oedipus. The incident of the Sphinx is of no dramatic importance in the play of Sophocles, being, in fact, only briefly alluded to by the chorus. Sophocles adapted the traditional myth to his own dramatic ends and the result was a profound tragedy with its own kind of "truth." The Sophoclean play, rather than the original myth, was the starting point of Freud's theory of the Oedipus complex.

4. Willetts, p. 108. It is also worth noting that there is another parallel between the Bronze Age calendar of Knossos and the calendar of eighth century Boeotia familiar to Hesiod. According to Hesiod, certain days of the month are especially holy and are lucky or unlucky for various purposes. Among them he names the fourth, the tenth, the eleventh, the twelfth, the thirteenth and the fourteenth. (Hesiod, "Works and Days," *The Homeric Hymns and Homerica,* trans. H. G. Evelyn-White, Cambridge, Mass.: Harvard University Press, 1967, pp. 59-63.) A parallel can be seen in a Linear B tablet from Knossos (V 280) which appears to designate certain days in the month of Wo-de-wi-jo which are holy and upon which certain actions should not be performed. They are the fourth, the tenth, the eleventh, the twelfth, the thirteenth and the fourteenth corresponding with the days mentioned by Hesiod. (Ventris and Chadwick, *Documents in Mycenaean Greek,* p. 311.)

5. Pierre Grimal, ed., *Larousse World Mythology* (London: The Hamlyn Publishing Group Ltd., 1971), p. 168.

6. Arthur Bernard Cook, *Zeus* (New York: Biblo and Tannen, 1964), I, p. 421.

7. Graves, *Greek Myths,* I, p. 122 and II, p. 80.

8. Graves, *Greek Myths,* I, p. 125.

9. Stylianou Alexiou, *Guide to the Archaeological Museum of Heraclion* (Athens: General Direction of Antiquities and Restoration, 1968), p. 101.

10. Graves, *Greek Myths,* II, pp. 49-50.

11. Graves, *Greek Myths,* II, p. 50.

12. Graves, *Greek Myths,* I, pp. 237-245.

13. Graves, *Greek Myths,* I, pp. 127-130.

14. Mario Moretti, *The National Museum of Villa Giulia* (Rome: Tipografia Artistica Editrice, A. Nardini, n.d.), p. 104.

CHAPTER IV

1. Graves, *Greek Myths,* II, pp. 229-230.

2. Graves, *Greek Myths,* I, p. 331.

3. Spyridon Marinatos, "Thera, Key to the Riddle of Minos," *National Geographic,* Vol. 141, No. 5, May, 1972, pp. 702-726.

4. Graves, *Greek Myths,* I, p. 171.

5. Cook, I, pp. 107-108.

6. Graves, *Greek Myths,* II, p. 225.

7. Paul MacKendrick, *The Mute Stones Speak* (New York: The New American Library, 1960), p. 38.

8. Cook II, p. 654.

9. This equivalence was first pointed out by Sir Arthur Evans, *The*

Journal of Hellenic Studies, 1901, XXI, p. 108.

10. Sir James George Frazer, *Pausanias's Description of Greece* (New York: Macmillan and Co., Ltd., 1965), I, p. 519.

11. Samuel Noah Kramer, *The Sumerians* (Chicago: University of Chicago Press, 1964), p. 91.

CHAPTER V

1. Vermeule, p. 294.

2. Graves, *Greek Myths,* I, p. 55.

3. Cook, I, pp. 175–176.

4. Graves, *Greek Myths,* I, p. 303.

5. C. G. Jung, "The Spirit Mercurius," *Alchemical Studies, The Collected Works of C.G. Jung,* XIII, (New York: The Princeton University Press, 1956), *passim.*

6. Graves, *Greek Myths,* I, p. 65.

7. Cook, II, p. 1130.

8. Cook, II, p. 563.

9. Graves, *Greek Myths,* I, p. 65.

10. Strong, p. 29.

11. Graves, *Greek Myths,* I, p. 56.

12. Cook, II, p. 450.

13. Cook, II, p. 989.

14. Graves, *Greek Myths,* II, p. 381.

15. Cook, II, pp. 611–612.

16. Gordon H. Clark, *Selections from Hellenistic Philosophy* (New York: F. S. Crofts and Co., 1940), pp. 184-191.

17. Clark, pp. 184–218.

18. Cook, II, p. 613; quotation from Hermes Trismegistus.

19. Ventris and Chadwick, pp. 463–464.

20. Ventris and Chadwick, p. 459.

21. Ventris and Chadwick, p. 463.

22. Ventris and Chadwick, p. 286.

23. Vermeule, pp. 292–294.

24. Ventris and Chadwick, p. 288.

25. Ventris and Chadwick, p. 463.

26. R.W. Hutchinson, *Prehistoric Crete* (Middlesex, England: Penguin Books Ltd., 1968), p. 208.

27. Graves, *Greek Myths,* I, p. 67.

28. Hesiod, "Works and Days," *The Homeric Hymns and Homerica,* trans. H.G. Evelyn-White (Cambridge, Mass.: Harvard University Press, 1967), p. 37.

29. R.W. Hutchinson, p. 38.

30. Graves, *White Goddess,* p. 248.

31. Cook, II, p. 240.

32. Graves, *Greek Myths,* I, p. 56.

33. Graves, *Greek Myths,* I, p. 28.

34. Cook, II, pp. 996–999.

35. Harold Bayley, *The Lost Language of Symbolism* (London: Williams and Norgate, 1968), pp. 145-146; Quotation from Chrysostom.

Chapter VI

1. Graves, *Greek Myths*, I, pp. 138–139.
2. Cook, I, pp. 70–81.
3. Jones, *Strabo*, II, p. 343.
4. Graves, *Greek Myths*, I, p. 140.
5. Homer, *The Odyssey*, trans. E. V. Rieu (Harmondsworth, Middlesex, England: Penguin Books Ltd., 1955), p. 292.
6. Jones, *Strabo*, II, p. 345; quotation from Hesiod.
7. Cook, I, p. 79, notes 10 and 12.
8. Frazer, *Pausanias*, I, pp. 374–375.
9. Frazer, *Pausanias*, I, p. 374.
10. Cook, I, pp. 80–81.
11. Cook, I, pp. 343–344.
12. Frazer, *Pausanias*, I, p. 27.

Chapter VII

1. Graves, *Greek Myths*, I, pp. 263–268.
2. Graves, *Greek Myths*, II, p. 399.
3. Graves, *Greek Myths*, I, pp. 266–267.
4. Graves, *Greek Myths*, I, p. 185.
5. Frazer, *Pausanias*, I, pp. 260–261.
6. Ludwig Drees, *Olympia* (New York: Frederick A. Praeger 1968), p. 12.
7. F. M. Cornford, "The Origin of the Olympic Games," in J. E. Harrison, *Themis* (Cleveland: World Publishing Co., 1962), p. 240.
8. Cornford, p. 239.
9. Frazer, *Pausanias*, I, p. 260.
10. Frazer, *Pausanias*, I, p. 261.
11. Cornford, p. 236.
12. Cornford, p. 225.
13. Cornford, p. 230.
14. Graves, *Greek Myths*, II, p. 34.
15. Myrtilus, according to myth, was the son of Hermes. His involvement in the death of the sacred king at the solstice is therefore understandable. Functioning for his father, Hermes, he is responsible for the death of the old king and the advent of the new king. Graves, *Greek Myths*, II, p. 33.
16. Graves, *White Goddess*, p. 196.
17. Graves, *Greek Myths*, II, p. 33.
18. Johann Jakob Bachofen calls attention to a number of myths in which a sun-hero races a moon-maiden to win her as a bride. He writes, "Herein lies the root of the often recurring mythological fiction of the

Amazonian virgin who races with the hero and is carried off as the prize of his victory." J.J. Bachofen, *Myth, Religion, and Mother Right* (Princeton: Princeton University Press, New Jersey, 1967), p. 177.

CHAPTER VIII

1. Cook, I, pp. 412–413.

2. Graves, *Greek Myths,* I, pp. 292–294.

3. Cook, I, p. 413, note 2.

4. Graves, *Greek Myths,* II, pp. 44–45.

5. Cook, I, p. 106.

6. Cook, I, p. 106.

7. Graves, *Greek Myths,* I, p. 347.

8. Tom Peete Cross and Clark Harris Slover, *Ancient Irish Tales* (New York: Barnes and Noble, 1969), p. 588.

9. Graves, *White Goddess,* p. 248.

10. Graves, *White Goddess,* pp. 38–40.

11. Cross and Slover, p. 595.

12. Graves, *White Goddess,* pp. 88–89.

13. For a discussion of the possible historical aspect of the Theseus myth, see *The Thread of Ariadne,* Chapter VII.

14. Cook. I, p. 474, note 1.

15. Cook, I, p. 475.

16. Graves, *White Goddess,* p. 187; quotation from Lucian.

17. Sir Arthur Evans, *Archaeologia,* 2nd series, XV, 1913–14. *passim.*

18. A labyrinth of this type, which is possibly older, is inscribed on a stone found in Ireland. This "Hollywood Stone," as it is called, is discussed by L. J. D. Richardson, who infers that it may have been the work of Bronze Age "travelling craftsmen of ultimately Minoan or Mycenaean origin." L. J. D. Richardson, "The Labyrinth," *Proceedings of the Cambridge Colloquium on Mycenaean Studies* (Cambridge, 1966), pp. 295-296.

19. L. J. D. Richardson, pp. 290–291.

20. L. J. D. Richardson, p. 293.

21. John W. Layard, *Stone Men of Malekula* (London: Chatto and Windus, 1942), p. 652.

22. Cook, II, pp. 601–610.

CHAPTER IX

1. Oswald Spengler, "Meaning of Numbers," *The Decline of the West,* in *The World of Mathematics,* ed., James R. Newman (New York: Simon and Schuster, 1956), p. 2315.

2. Bayley, p. 146.

3. *The Oxford English Dictionary,* Vol. I (Oxford: Oxford University Press, 1933), p. 32. According to the *O. E. D.,* Abracadabra occurs first in a poem by Q. Severus Sammonicus in the second century A.D., but its ultimate origin is unknown. *Abraxas* is said to be the name of the supreme deity of

the Gnostic sect of Basilides, who equated it by number symbolism with 365. *O. E. D.*, Vol. I, p. 32. Dr. Ernest Klein, citing Irenaeus, gives the number symbolism of *Abraxas* as follows: a = 1, b = 2, r = 100, a = 1, x = 60, a = 1, s = 200. Total = 365. *A Comprehensive Etymological Dictionary of the English Language*, Vol. I (New York, 1966), p. 6. Gertrude Jobes traces *Abraxas* to the Persian sun-god, Mithras, and equates it with *Abracadabra* because both words are symbolically equal to 365. *Dictionary of Mythology, Folklore, and Symbols*, Part I (New York: The Scarecrow Press, 1962), p. 19. Considering all these sources, it appears that *Abraxas* may have been the root of *Abracadabra*, but this is a conjecture rather than a certainty.

4. Dr. Ernest Klein, *A Comprehensive Etymological Dictionary of the English Language*, Vol. I (New York: Elsevier Publishing Co., 1966), p. 6.

5. Cook, I, p. 517.

6. *The Oxford English Dictionary*, Vol. I, p. 31.

7. Strong, pp. 129–131.

8. Strong, p. 130.

9. Max Büdinger, "Die römischen Spiele und der Patriciat," *Sitzungsberichte der Philosophisch—Historischen Classe der Kaiserlichen Akademie der Wissenschaften* (Vienna, 1891), Vol. 123, pp. 47–55.

10. Emeline Richardson, *The Etruscans* (Chicago: University of Chicago Press, 1964), p. 220.

11. Jacques Heurgon, *Daily Life of the Etruscans* (New York: The Macmillan Co., 1964), p. 183.

12. Heurgon, pp. 184–185.

13. Graves, *White Goddess*, p. 316.

14. Graves, *Greek Myths*, I, pp. 52–53.

15. Strong, p. 94.

16. Jane Ellen Harrison, *Themis* (New York: World Publishing Co., 1962), p. 198.

17. MacKendrick, p. 54.

18. Emeline Richardson, p. 219.

19. Graves, *White Goddess*, p. 198.

20. Cook, II, p. 339, note 4.

21. Heurgon, pp. 184–185.

22. Willetts, pp. 92–99.

23. Graves, *White Goddess*, p. 242.

24. Strong, p. 134.

25. Emeline Richardson, p. 2.

26. Alexiou, p. 56 and Hutchinson, p. 183.

27. Graves, *White Goddess*, p. 297.

28. J. D. S. Pendlebury, *The Archaeology of Crete* (New York: W.W. Norton and Co., 1965), p. 146.

29. Alexiou, p. 56.

30. Pendlebury, p. 167.

31. R. W. Hutchinson, p. 192.

32. Pendlebury, p. 167.

33. According to Hans Georg Wunderlich an Egyptian board game is described in a papyrus of the XII Dynasty (and, hence, contemporary with the Knossos game board) which was played by two players but not as an

amusement. On the contrary, the papyrus makes it clear that what was at stake was nothing less than bliss in the hereafter for the winner and death for the loser. Hans Georg Wunderlich, *The Secret of Crete* (Fontana/Collins, Glasgow, Scotland, 1976), p. 224.

34. Dr. Marie-Louise von Franz, *Man and His Symbols,* ed. by Carl G. Jung (New York: Doubleday and Co., Inc., 1964), p. 310.

Bibliography

Alexiou, Stylianou. *Guide to the Archaeological Museum of Heraclion*. Athens: General Direction of Antiquities and Restoration, 1968.

Atkinson, R. J. C. *Stonehenge*. London: Pelican Books, 1960.

Bayley, Harold. *The Lost Language of Symbolism*. London: Williams and Norgate, 1968.

Blegen, Carl W. *Troy and the Trojans*. New York: Frederick A. Praeger, 1963.

Branigan, Keith. *The Tombs of Mesara*. London: Duckworth, 1970.

Brunés, Tons. *The Secrets of Ancient Geometry*. 2 vols. Copenhagen: Rhodos, 1967.

Büdinger, Max. "Die römischen Spiele und der Patriciat," *Sitzungsberichte der Philosophisch-Historischen Akademie der Wissenschaften* Vol. 123: (Vienna 1891). 47–55.

Burn, Robert Andrew. *The World of Hesiod*. London: K. Paul, Trench, Trubner & Co., Ltd., 1936.

Cameron, Mark, and Sinclair Hood. *Sir Arthur Evans' Knossos Fresco Atlas*. Farnborough: Gregg Press, 1967.

Campbell, Joseph. *The Masks of God: Primitive Mythology*. New York: The Viking Press, 1968.

Campbell, Joseph. *The Masks of God: Occidental Mythology*. New York: The Viking Press, 1969.

Campbell, Joseph. *The Masks of God: Oriental Mythology*. New York: The Viking Press, 1969.

Casson, Stanley. *Ancient Cyprus*. Westport, Conn: Greenwood Press. 1970.

Chadwick, John. *The Decipherment of Linear B*. Cambridge: The Cambridge University Press, 1970.

Coarelli, Filippo, ed. *Le Città Etrusche*. Florence: Arnoldo Mandadori, 1973.

Cook, Arthur Bernard. *Zeus, A Study in Ancient Religion*. 2 vols. New York: Biblo and Tannen, 1965.

Cook, J. M. *The Greeks in Ionia and the East*. New York: Frederick A. Praeger, 1963.

Clark, Gordon H. *Selections from Hellenistic Philosophy*. New York: F. S. Crofts and Co., 1940.

Cross, Tom Peete, and Clark Harris Slover. *Ancient Irish Tales*. New York: Barnes and Noble, 1969.

Diodorus Siculus. *Works*. 12 vols., trans. C. H. Oldfather. Cambridge: Harvard University Press, 1961.

Drees, Ludwig. *Olympia*. New York: Frederick A. Praeger, 1968.

Dyer, James. *Discovering Archaeology in England and Wales*. Tring, Herts.: Shire Publications, 1969.

Eliade, Mircea. *The Myth of the Eternal Return*. New York: Pantheon Books, 1954.

Evans, Sir Arthur. *The Palace of Minos*. 7 vols. London: Macmillan Co., 1930.

Forsdyke, John. *Greece Before Homer*. New York: W. W. Norton and Co., 1964.

Fowler, W. Warde. *The Roman Festivals of the Period of the Republic*. Port Washington, New York: Kennikat Press, 1969.

Frankfort, Henri, H. A. Frankfort, John Wilson, and Thorkild Jacobsen. *Before Philosophy*. Middlesex, England: Penguin Books, 1961.

Frankfort, Henri. *The Birth of Civilization in the Near East*. New York: Barnes and Noble, 1968.

Frankfort, Henri. *Kingship and the Gods*. Chicago: University of Chicago Press, 1965.

Frazer, Sir James George. *The Golden Bough*. London: Macmillan and Co., Ltd., 1929.

Frazer, Sir James George. *Pausanias's Description of Greece*. 6 vols. New York: Macmillan and Co., Ltd., 1965.

Frazer, Sir James George. *Graecia Antiqua*. Ann Arbor, Michigan: University Microfilms, 1970.

Glasgow, George. *The Minoans*. Port Washington, New York: Kennikat Press, 1969.

Graham, James Walter. *The Palaces of Crete,* Princeton: Princeton University Press, 1962.

Graves, Robert. *The White Goddess*. New York: Random House, 1948.

Graves, Robert. *The Greek Myths*. 2 vols. Middlesex, England: Penguin Books Ltd., 1969.

Grimal, Pierre. ed. *Larousse World Mythology*. London: The Hamlyn Publishing Group, Ltd., 1971.

Guthrie, W. K. C. *A History of Greek Philosophy*. vol. I. Cambridge: Cambridge University Press, 1962.

Harrison, Jane Ellen. *Themis*. Cleveland: World Publishing Co., 1962.

Hawkes, Jacquetta. *Dawn of the Gods.* New York: Random House, 1968.

Hawkins, Gerald S. *Stonehenge Decoded.* New York: Dell Publishing Co., 1965.

Herberger, Charles F. *The Thread of Ariadne: The Labyrinth of the Calendar of Minos.* New York: Philosophical Library, 1972.

Hesiod. *Works and Days.* trans. Hugh G. Evelyn-White. Cambridge, Mass.: Harvard University Press, 1967.

Heurgon, Jacques. *Daily Life of the Etruscans.* New York: The Macmillan Co., 1964.

Homer. *The Iliad.* trans. Sir William Marris. Oxford: Oxford University Press, 1934.

Homer. *The Odyssey.* trans. E. V. Rieu. Middlesex, England: Penguin Books, Ltd., 1955.

Hooke, S. H. ed. *Myth, Ritual, and Kingship.* Oxford: The Clarendon Press, 1958.

Hutchinson, G. Evelyn. "Long Meg Reconsidered," I and II, *American Scientist.* vol. 60, no. 1 and 2 (Mar.-April, 1972).

Hutchinson, R. W. *Prehistoric Crete.* Middlesex, England, Penguin Books Ltd., 1968.

Ingersoll, Ernest. *Birds in Legend, Fable, and Folklore.* New York: Longmans, Green, 1923.

James, E. O. *Prehistoric Religion.* New York: Barnes and Noble, 1957.

James, E. O. *The Cult of the Mother-Goddess.* New York: Barnes and Noble, 1959.

Jones, H. L. trans. *The Geography of Strabo.* 8 vols. Cambridge, Mass.: Harvard University Press, 1961.

Jung, Carl G. *Psyche and Symbol.* New York: Doubleday and Co., 1958.

Jung, Carl G. ed. *Man and His Symbols.* Garden City, New York: Doubleday and Co., 1964.

Kenna, V. E. G. *Cretan Seals.* Oxford: Oxford University Press, 1960.

Kramer, Samuel Noah. *The Sumerians.* Chicago: University of Chicago Press, 1964.

Layard, John W. *Stone Men of Malekula.* London: Layard, Chatto and Windus, 1942.

Lévi-Strauss, Claude. *The Savage Mind.* Chicago: University of Chicago Press, 1966.

Littleton, C. Scott. *The New Comparative Mythology.* Berkeley: University of California Press, 1966.

Macalister, R. A. S. *The Archaeology of Ireland.* New York: Benjamin Blom, Inc., 1972.

MacKendrick, Paul. *The Greek Stones Speak.* New York: St. Martin's Press, 1962.

216

MacKendrick, Paul. *The Mute Stones Speak*. New York: The New American Library, 1966.

Mackenzie, Donald A. *The Migration of Symbols*. New York: Knopf, 1926.

Marinatos, Spyridon and Max Hirmer. *Crete and Mycenae*. New York: Abrams, 1960.

Marinatos, Spyridon. "Thera, Key to the Riddle of Minos," *National Geographic*. vol. 141, no. 5 (May 1972), 702-726.

Marshack, Alexander. *The Roots of Civilization*. New York: McGraw-Hill, 1972.

Marshack, Alexander. "Exploring the Mind of Ice Age Man," *National Geographic*. vol. 147, no. 1 (January 1975), 62-89.

McDonald, W. A. *Progress into the Past*. Bloomington, Indiana: Indiana University Press, 1969.

Mellersh, H. E. L. *Minoan Crete*. New York: G. P. Putnam's Sons, 1967.

Mingazzini, Paolino. *Greek Pottery Painting*. London: The Hamlyn Publishing Group, 1969.

Moretti, Mario. *The National Museum of Villa Giulia*. Rome: Tipografia Artistica Editrice, A. Nardini, n.d.

Mosso, A. *The Palaces of Crete and Their Builders*. London: T. F. Unwin, 1907.

Mylonas, George E. *Ancient Mycenae*. Princeton: Princeton University Press, 1957.

Neumann, Erich. *The Origins and History of Consciousness*. New York: Pantheon Books, 1964.

Neumann, Erich. *The Great Mother*. Princeton: Princeton University Press, 1970.

Newall, R. S. *Stonehenge*. London: Her Majesty's Stationery Office, 1959.

Newman, James R. *The World of Mathematics*. 4 vols. New York: Simon and Schuster, 1956.

Nilsson, Martin P. *Primitive Time-Reckoning*. Lund: C. W. K. Gleerup, 1920.

Nilsson, Martin, P. *Cults, Myths, Oracles, and Politics in Ancient Greece*. New York: Cooper Square Publishers, 1972.

Nilsson, Martin P. *The Minoan Mycenaean Religion*. Lund: C. W. K. Gleerup, 1950.

Nilsson, Martin P. *A History of Greek Religion*. Oxford: Clarendon Press, 1967.

Nilsson, Martin P. *The Mycenaean Origin of Greek Mythology*. New York: W. W. Norton and Co., 1963.

O'Riordain, Sean P. and Glyn Daniel. *New Grange*. New York: Frederick A. Praeger, 1964.

Palmer, Leonard R. *A New Guide to the Palace of Knossos.* New York: Frederick A. Praeger, 1969.

Parke, H. W. *Greek Oracles.* Cambridge, Mass.: Harvard University Press, 1967.

Parrot, André. *Babylon and the Old Testament.* New York: Philosophical Library, 1958.

Pendlebury, J. D. S. *The Archaeology of Crete.* New York: W. W. Norton and Co., 1965.

Procopiou, Angelo. *Athens, City of the Gods.* New York: Stein and Day, 1964.

Richardson, Emeline. *The Etruscans.* Chicago: University of Chicago Press, 1964.

Richardson, L. J. D. "The Labyrinth," *Proceedings of the Cambridge Colloquium on Mycenaean Studies.* Cambridge, 1966.

Sakellariou, Agnes and George Papathanasopoulos. *Guide to National Archaeological Museum, Prehistoric Collections.* Athens: Department of Antiquities and Restoration, 1965.

Samuel, Alan E. *The Mycenaeans in History.* Englewood Cliffs, New Jersey: Prentice-Hall, 1966.

Sarton, George. *A History of Science.* Cambridge, Mass.: Harvard University Press, 1959.

Stenico, Arturo. *Roman and Etruscan Painting.* New York: The Viking Press, 1963.

Strong, Donald. *The Early Etruscans.* New York: G. P. Putnam's Sons, 1968.

Taylour, Lord William. *The Mycenaeans.* New York: Frederick A. Praeger, 1964.

Van Gennup, A. *The Rites of Passage.* Chicago: University of Chicago Press, 1960.

Ventris, Michael, and Chadwick, John. *Documents in Mycenaean Greek.* Cambridge: Cambridge University Press, 1973.

Vermeule, Emily. *Greece in the Bronze Age.* Chicago: University of Chicago Press, 1967.

Virgil. *Aeneid.* trans. W. F. Jackson Knight. Middlesex, England: Penguin Books, Ltd., 1968.

Wace, Helen. *Mycenae Guide.* Meriden, Conn.: The Meriden Gravure Co., 1969.

Willetts, R. F. *Cretan Cults and Festivals.* New York: Barnes and Noble, 1962.

Willetts, R. F. *Ancient Crete.* London: Routledge and K. Paul, 1965.

Wunderlich, Hans Georg. *The Secret of Crete.* Glasgow, Scotland: Fontana/Collins, 1976.